THE ENGLISH LEGACY

THE ENGLISH LEGACY

Norman Renshaw

Book Guild Publishing
Sussex, England

First published in Great Britain in 2009 by
The Book Guild Ltd
Pavilion View
19 New Road
Brighton, BN1 1UF

Typesetting in Times by
Keyboard Services, Luton, Bedfordshire

Printed in Great Britain by
CPI Antony Rowe

A catalogue record for this book is available from
The British Library

ISBN 978 1 84624 331 8

Contents

Introduction

An attempt is made in the following pages to present some aspects of the development and history of England and the English people, and their contribution to the world at large. It does, however, contain many of the basic facts of history, which I believe are necessary for any pupil, as a grounding before deeper study begins.

The Normans were not the beginning of England's monarchy as some seem to believe. England today is still divided and administered much as the Saxons decreed, evidenced by the shire system and the shire courts. Even the laws later exerted in the twelfth century by Henry II were a regurgitated version of those introduced by Alfred in the ninth century. The sequential aspect is emphasised because the teaching in our schools is invariably patchy and disjointed, with continuity being almost non-existent. A lesson on the Roman occupation might be followed in the next session by the reign of Henry VIII or the Norman Conquest – confusing, even if the content of the particular session was absorbing. The narrative concerning monarchy terminates at the death of Elizabeth I at which point the crown ceased to be English and became British.

Some have questioned the relevance of history. The great motor car innovator Henry Ford reportedly once said 'history is more or less bunk'. He now seems to be isolated in this view. It is discounted by every country in the world as they exhibit pride in their past. The demand for books and films with a historical basis continues unabated. Love of the past is embedded deep within the human psyche and has an impact on almost everyone. Could anyone visit Hadrian's Wall and be indifferent to its atmosphere, or meander through the remains of the Roman castle at Sandwich in Kent, where vestiges of possibly the first Roman road in England are still visible, and be unmoved? England has a wealth of similar sites dotted all over the country. The French in their Revolution murdered their despised aristocracy who inhabited magnificent châteaux but nowadays maintain these buildings with reverence because, good or bad, they represent their collective past. Hundreds of thousands of foreign visitors visit them every year, generating valuable income from the tourist industry. We are fortunate in England to have organisations like English Heritage and The National Trust who have supervised the restoration of great houses or castles now open to the public, enabling them to experience vicarious sensations from the past.

In paying homage to our outstanding forebears one should spare a moment to reflect that among those mentioned there might be found a distant ancestor of one's own. It is not beyond the bounds of possibility. In these days of computer assisted searching for family origins it is within the compass of almost everyone to access this information and there are organisations continually adding to the existing records. Should it happen that a family link is found, no matter how tenuous or far distant, it could be like sharing an almost mystical experience. This is not merely fanciful or idle speculation. During the celebrations of 2005 to mark the 200th anniversary of the Battle of Trafalgar, there were hundreds of people lining the harbours at Portsmouth who were able to prove kinship with Admiral Nelson or others who took part in the struggle. Many others experienced the pride of having a traceable family relationship with crew members who had also served aboard HMS *Victory*.

This kinship may even reach back to the great English adventurers and seafarers like Drake, Raleigh, Anson, Gilbert, Franklin, Hudson and Cook who were instrumental in discovering and establishing trade links with many parts of the world. The early trading links became settlements and then colonies. They were established by the English, eventually growing in size and importance until they became part of an empire. The earliest recorded attempt at English colonisation of North America was in 1584 by an expedition headed by Walter Raleigh. There was a difference in purpose in the American experience which was undertaken not for trade, but settlement. Although not immediately successful it provided vital information about the region, better enabling later emigrants to deal with problems they would inevitably encounter. The eventual success of the English/American settlers to the point where they set up their own government, independent of the mother country but embodying its democratic principles, attracting people from all across Europe to this New World.

On the subject of history, we have never been better served than we are today in the numbers of expert historians publishing their works. The nature of their approach seems to be more analytical and written with more freedom than in the past. This could be because earlier recording of history took place under the gaze of repressive sovereigns and had to conform to the royal view. The style of the modern writer offers a wider scope to those who wish to read for enjoyment as well as for the purpose of study.

Anyone who might have reservations about reading history should bear in mind that it is entirely based on facts and events. The heroism, bravery, cowardice, deceit, murder and intrigue, both political and sexual, were part and parcel of the narrative of the times and are not exclusive to one country or nation, but part of human nature.

1

The Arrival of the Founders

Substantial numbers of migrants have been entering Britain for thousands of years. Modern archaeologists have uncovered detailed evidence of the existence of cultures going back at least 25,000 years. Traces of the Bronze Age civilisation which followed them are easily identifiable through their tools and weapons. Each successive incomer cultivated the soil and grew several types of cereal and grain crops, including wheat, and were also skilful weavers.

There were apparently three waves of Celtic invaders who came from Central Europe, some of whom either moved on or were ousted by those arriving later. The last of these were known as the Belgae and were inhabiting the south-east of Britain when the Romans first landed, led by Julius Caesar. The Celts had conquered the Bronze Age people, who were evidently the dominant culture. In common with most victorious invaders it is entirely possible that the people who previously occupied the country were not entirely eliminated but either used as slaves or absorbed into the new society. This would have been the most likely approach, if only to take advantage of valuable local knowledge. Details of crops which could be successfully grown and wildlife to hunt would also be essential information for the newcomers and another practical reason for absorbing them into a new society rather than eliminating them.

Although the Welsh people generally refer to themselves as the original Britons there is no doubt that the country was already populated when they too arrived here as invaders, which invalidates this claim. All of these early settlers were essentially tribal groups and their decline as the major influence began with the arrival of the Romans.

The Roman incursion began in 55 BC when Julius Caesar landed with an expeditionary force near Deal in Kent. This first exploratory invasion lasted barely a month, but Caesar had been shown that he needed a substantial force if he were to make real inroads against stern opposition. After a winter of planning and preparation he returned in the summer of 54 BC. With a powerful force he made fairly quick progress, reaching north of London where he defeated the warlord Cassivelaunus who agreed henceforth to pay tribute. Having established the fact that he had added Britain to the Roman Empire Caesar was gone again by September. The whole purpose of this exercise was to draw attention to himself in Rome by adding to his credibility as a potential leader via expansion of the Empire. This enabled him to face the Senate to bid for his ultimate goal which was head of the Roman state. Britain was left in peace by Rome for a century afterwards but the links made with the Roman-dominated Continent continued to blossom.

The Emperor Claudius decided in AD 43 to send another army to Britain, this time to subdue the country and make it a recognised province of Rome, with all the concomitant trappings and responsibilities, particularly taxes. He was already the figurehead of Rome, but his position had become a bit shaky and he needed a victory to convince the citizenry that he was still a strong leader. His colossal army, reputed to exceed 40,000, was placed under the command of Aulus Plautius, who drove through as far as the Thames, waiting there by arrangement until Claudius was able to join him in the campaign to take Colchester (Camulodunum). All the spadework had already been done by Plautius and his troops, but by arriving at the apparent moment of victory, the impression was given that Claudius had masterminded the whole episode. The Celtic army was routed and thousands of prisoners taken. It was, in a political sense, largely a cosmetic exercise, orchestrated in such a way as to enable Claudius to re-enter Rome in the guise of a conquering hero. This is indicated by the fact that his stay in Britain amounted to a mere 16 days.

It was another distinguished general – Vespasian – who was entrusted with the task of conquering the tribes in the south-west. A ruthless and resourceful soldier, he too succeeded in realising his ambition in becoming emperor 25 years later. It seemed that Britain had become the proving ground for budding emperors. Incidentally, Vespasian was the man responsible for the beginning of the building of the Colosseum in Rome, started in AD 72 and finished by Titus in AD 80, and originally known as the Flavian Amphitheatre.

One of the main Celtic figures of the period was Caractacus, who escaped from Colchester and took up arms against the Romans, but was finally captured and sent to Rome. Another was Boudicca (or Boadicea), who led the tribes in rebellion, razed Colchester to the ground and killed all the Roman occupants and their Celtic adherents, repeating this devastation in St Albans and London. A lack of a cohesive plan to keep the tribes supplied with regular provisions and in close formation caused their downfall. When the main Roman army under Paulinus caught up with them, they had become fragmented and disorganised. They were in no condition to resist an enemy whose discipline was immaculate. The result was a massacre. The magnitude and ferocity of the havoc wrought by Boudicca and her army did have a positive side; it caused the Roman authorities to reconsider their treatment of the people and a more just system of governing was instituted.

In AD 136 Emperor Hadrian had a wall built across the

country between Carlisle and the River Tyne near Newcastle. In AD 142 Emperor Antoninus Pius built a second wall further north, connecting the Firth of Clyde and the Firth of Forth in Scotland. Remains of both can still be seen. Both walls came under continuous attack from north and south. In the extreme north the Picts and Saxons obviously cooperated because Claudian, the Roman historian, writing in the fourth century, refers to Theodosius attacking Picts and Saxons in Orkney and Shetland. In the south the Brigantes carried out constant assaults. The Picts were the most populous of all the northern tribes until the tenth century when they were ousted by the Scots, from Ireland. The mystery surrounding the Picts is the sudden disappearance of their culture from Britain after the Scots under McAlpin took the crown in the tenth century. After all, they were the ancient people whose prehistoric settlements, brochs and other relics are the definitive historical evidence throughout the north of what is now Scotland, Orkney and Shetland, and traces of them can be found in the south as far as Wigtonshire and Berwickshire.

When finally the decadence of the Roman Empire caused it to implode and the armies were required to return from the outposts of the Empire to defend their homeland, an opportunity came the way of another group of people looking for land. After the withdrawal of the powerful Roman forces, those left behind presented a much softer target and they came under attack almost immediately. These new invaders were Germanic peoples from tribes such as the Angles, Jutes and Saxons, closely related to one another and speaking roughly a common language. Their conquest of England began about the middle of the fourth century and was probably completed a little over a century later. It was made easier as a result of the defensive vacuum created by the withdrawal of the Romans. The most vulnerable were the Romanised Celts of the south, particularly in Kent and Essex. The western Celts and Picts also saw the evacuation of the Roman legions as an opportunity to take advantage of the situation but they too fell victim to the invading Saxon hordes.

Roman civilization in Britain had been well founded by this time and Vortigern, the Celtic leader who, in former days, would have been the king in every sense of the word, had become little more than a governor under Roman control. Military affairs would not have come under his jurisdiction, therefore after Rome's departure, if he wanted to survive, he was forced to seek an alliance elsewhere. This he managed somehow to achieve with the Jutish invaders led by Horsa and Hengist (or Hengest), whereby they would act as mercenaries in defence of the south east in exchange for a grant of land. According to the writings of the Venerable Bede they landed at Ebbsfleet in Kent and after they were victorious in at least two battles it is said that Vortigern granted them Essex and Sussex – but judging by the fact that between Christchurch in Hampshire and Bournemouth there is a headland which after more than 1,500 years is still named Hengistbury Head one can be fairly sure that they controlled a far greater area than the piece of territory originally granted. Ultimately they became the dominant force in the south east in spite of the original intention of Vortigern to employ them as a glorified bodyguard. It should be remembered that Hengist was a formidable warrior with a reputation causing him to be mentioned in the great saga *Beowulf*, and therefore, in a violent age, he was someone unlikely to accept control by anyone.

The mistake made by Vortigern was that by making the Norsemen indispensable to his security he rendered himself expendable. He did take the precaution to hedge his bets by marrying the daughter of Hengist which, although the Norse warriors still usurped his kingdom, probably saved his life.

From then on the encroachment of the Angles, Saxons and Jutes continued until, by the end of the sixth century, they had covered and settled the whole of what is now

England and Scotland as far as the Firth of Forth. Over the years they became a more civilised society, converted to Christianity and developed laws and legal procedures ahead of their European counterparts. The northern area known as Bernicia became part of Northumbria, ruled by King Edwin who founded the city of Edinburgh. The Northumbrians developed quite early into a very powerful Anglo-Saxon settlement. They had brought with them improved agricultural methods, one of which was the introduction of the plough. Over time, little kingdoms evolved probably for localised defence and by the early seventh century, seven were recognisable: Wessex, Sussex, Kent, Essex, East Anglia, Mercia and Northumbria. Of these, Mercia, Northumbria and Wessex emerged as the three dominant kingdoms. We know from surviving records that there was further competition among these remaining societies. Not least of those with territorial ambitions were the powerful Northumbrians. In the seventh century this led them to attack the Mercian people of the Midlands of England.

Unexpectedly, the Northumbrians were defeated and their leader, the eponymous King Oswald (or Oswys), was killed in the battle which took place in Shropshire in AD 642. The site was named after the defeated king, and thereafter the battle was referred to as the battle of Oswys Tree. Probably a tree was planted there to commemorate the site. The town which later grew there became known as the town of Oswestry.

The effects of this defeat left the north-east coast at the mercy of the pagan Danes who intensified their policy of mindless devastation and slaughter. After a protracted period of intense attacks they then changed their policy. Instead of returning home, as they were wont to do in the past, their strategy changed to one of colonisation with the intention of spreading their control throughout the country. By being separated into seven little kingdoms, the Anglo-Saxons had left themselves vulnerable to these attacks and the Danes began picking them off one by one until only Wessex remained. The following kings led the revival and united the whole country under Saxon rule once more, remaining in power (except for a short period in 1014 and from 1017–1042) until the Norman invasion of 1066.

Saxon Kings

Egbert, King of Wessex, 802–839

Recognising the Danish tactics, Egbert sought to counteract them by uniting the remaining parts of the country. By conquest he brought the other kingdoms into subservience to his rule, thus becoming the first Saxon king whose leadership was generally accepted.

Ethelwulf, 839–857

Ethelwulf succeeded his father and spent practically his whole reign in repelling Danish incursions. He began a practice of making regular donations to support the clergy. This is believed to be the origin of the system of tithes. He had four children, the youngest of which was Alfred the Great.

Ethelbald, 858–860

Ethelbert, 860–866

Ethelred, 866–871

The three older brothers of Alfred were constantly engaged in a war of attrition with the invading Danes. The strain of defending a kingdom which had become isolated was obviously immense. It was made worse because it was against an enemy who were not only established on their doorstep but were bringing in fresh warriors all the time. Little wonder that none of them survived as king for more than six years, but they succeeded in holding the line until the arrival of Alfred.

Alfred the Great, 871–901

A most unusual man, a warrior, a scholar, a reformer and a visionary, Alfred not only fought for justice for his people but dispensed it to his enemies. The frequency of attacks on all parts of the country increased in this period as the Danes felt that the complete domination of the country was within their grasp. But for the intervention of King Alfred they might have succeeded. While fighting at the side of his brothers, Alfred had won victories and suffered defeats at the hands of these invaders. After the death of Ethelred I who succumbed to his wounds in the Battle of Ashdown in 871, he became king. At the age of 23 he had already fought nine pitched battles, some of which ended in stalemate or a temporary peace treaty, but Ashdown was the first in which the Danes had been completely routed. An oath meant nothing to these pagans and they broke them without compunction. If they were defeated they would plead for peace on oath but only to gain respite while they regrouped to launch another attack.

After the Danes dishonoured yet another treaty, Alfred's army was ambushed and almost destroyed. He and his surviving followers were reduced to living as fugitives in the marshes and swamps of Somerset until he could recruit more soldiers from the shires. His determination and skill as a war leader finally resulted in the utter defeat of the Danes in a defining battle. It took place in May 878 at Edington in Wiltshire and continued until these dedicated warriors begged for peace.

Alfred, apart from being a learned man, was also a realist who knew that more permanent solutions to establish continued peace had to be found, because the continuous warring between the various factions was destroying an otherwise prosperous country. He accomplished this after his victory over the Danish King Guthrum by extracting from him an oath of peace. More importantly, he persuaded him and his heathen countrymen to embrace Christianity. Alfred then secured Danish compliance by ceding to them lands in the eastern counties, where they settled to become part of England known as the Danelaw. Because of his outstanding qualities, Alfred the Great is worthy of separate study by people interested in English history. Apart from being a scholar he was a great soldier and far ahead of his time as a thinker, diplomat and humanitarian. He is buried in Winchester Cathedral and commemorated by a commanding statue in the middle of the town.

Surprisingly, in recent years, Alfred has been portrayed by at least one source as being something of a weakling on account of some abdominal complaint from which he suffered. An undiagnosed medical condition is on record as having affected him, making life even harder. That he endured 20 years or more of hard military campaigning and displayed a stubborn refusal ever to accept defeat does not sit well with the weakling theory, mentally, morally or physically. Remember too, he had finally defeated a massive Danish army and it was in his power to annihilate the remainder when he had them trapped, but he chose a route of forgiveness, baptism, concession, trust and diplomacy. Compassion on this scale was alien to the mentality of a ravaging killer like Guthrum and was almost unheard of in those times. The Danish leader was a superstitious person with fixed ideas of the world and after having been so decisively beaten he could not comprehend the concept of forgiveness. The conclusion he came to was that he had been heeding false gods. It was this prompting which induced him to accept the terms from Alfred, become a Christian and honour a pledge to keep his word. These incidents demonstrate the attributes possessed by Alfred which caused him to become the only British king to be accorded the title 'Great'. His *Book of Laws* laid the basis for English law, and many were retained by the Normans

Alfred was extraordinary in many ways but always alert to learning more from sources to which he might be exposed. When he was a boy and taken to Rome he presumably absorbed many lessons from their culture. His decision to fortify towns (burghs) possibly arose from those travels. He would have seen them as a common feature around Italy and the Mediterranean generally. Among his achievements was the decision to develop a naval fleet designed to counter the attacks by the Vikings in their fast oar-propelled boats. He reasoned that it was better to destroy these raiders at sea than to give them time to replenish their energies ashore. It would also protect the population and their food supplies from desecration. To do so the vessels he built had to be superior to those of either Danish or Frisian design. The boats he designed were nearly twice the length, sat higher in the water and accommodated proportionally more oarsmen. This provided the speed required to catch, ram and sink their opponents. Thus began the English Navy. Alfred's engagement at sea took place in AD 882, a matter of only four years after Edington.

There is an often told story about a time when Alfred was in exile and sheltering in a woodman's cottage. While preparing his bows and arrows and other weapons for the next encounter he forgot to look after the cakes as the cottager's wife had asked him to do, causing them to burn. It would be a pity if he should be remembered for a story of burnt cakes which was probably only recounted to emphasise the tragic depths to which Alfred's fortunes had plummeted at that time.

From a scholarly point of view, Alfred translated a number of works from Latin into Anglo-Saxon, including *Aesop's Fables*, Boetheius's *Consolation of Philosophy* and Bede's *Ecclesiastical History*. This clearly shows that his learning was far from being superficial. He also insisted that those among his countrymen who were elevated to positions of authority must learn to read, write and be capable of expressing themselves to their followers.

Edward the Elder, 901–925

Alfred's son Edward was an accomplished and hardened soldier who won many victories in the war of attrition against the Danes. During this period he continued the practice of fortifying towns. He subdued Northumbria and East Anglia and several of the Welsh tribes.

Athelstan, 925–940

Another great warrior leader, Athelstan was a grandson of Alfred the Great, and travelled the length and breadth of England from Land's End to the Firth of Forth establishing his royal authority and unifying England under the Saxon banner. Subsequently all the disaffected chieftains and kings gathered together in a great host to challenge this king. The combined forces of Olaf of Ireland, Vikings, Danes, Celts and Norwegians was led by Constantine of Scotland, who invaded England. Athelstan marched his army to meet them and challenged them to battle. It took place at a site called Brunanburgh in 937. The result was a resounding victory for Athelstan. (Although the site of this battle has never been accurately pinpointed by historians it is believed to be in the region of the Wirral in Cheshire. Interestingly, there is one place-name a few miles to the south of Edinburgh which tickles the imagination: 'Athelstaneford'.)

Athelstan died in approximately 940 leaving the country in a fairly prosperous and secure condition. Unfortunately, once he was out of the way Scandinavian attacks began again along the length of the east coast, but they never gained the same foothold as before. There followed a period when five kings ruled in quick succession.

Edmund I, 940–946

Brother of Athelstan and slain at a banquet on 26 May 946.

Edred, 946–955

Succeeded his brother Edmund and quelled Danes in Northumbria.

Edwy, 955–959

Supported the secular clergy against the monks. He incurred their enmity, causing Dunstan to incite a rebellion against him, driving him from the throne in favour of his brother Edgar.

Edgar, 959–975

Named 'The Peaceful' because of his concentration on civil and defensive military skills. One of the most distinguished of the Saxon kings he administered the kingdom vigorously and skilfully in matters both civil and military. He received ecclesiastical counsel and guidance from Dunstan, Archbishop of Canterbury, of whom he was also a great patron.

Edward the Martyr, 975–979

Edward was the victim of a treacherous and brutal murder planned by his stepmother and perpetrated by one of her servants. It made a deep impact on Saxon England, especially as at the time he was a guest at his stepmother's residence, Corfe Castle, in Dorset. As his stepmother had intended, it made way for her own son to take the throne. Her evil duplicity brought about an even worse problem for the country because her son Ethelred proved to be totally incapable of defending the country during a violent age.

Ethelred II, 979–1016

Nicknamed 'the Unready' or 'Unrede', Ethelred's every act demonstrated an inability to counter the threat of the Danes led by Sweyn Forkbeard. He tried to buy them off but his payments failed to pacify them because like all blackmailers they just asked for more. His next move was to effect a massacre of the Danes but this incited them to reply in AD 1013 with a consolidated attack, after which he was forced into exile. Sweyn immediately claimed the throne. After the death of Sweyn Ethelred was invited to return but his fortunes did not change for the better. He died during the struggle against Canute, the son of Sweyn, who was striving to take the place of his father.

Edmund II ('Ironside'), 1016–1017

Ethelred's eldest son. The war of attrition was engaged once more. Edmund defeated Canute in several battles and for the most part contained the Danish incursions. He was not able to repulse them altogether and lost the battle of Assandun in Essex which gave them possession of some lands in the Midlands and north. It was not until Edmund Ironside was assassinated in 1017 after a reign of only seven months that the way was clear for Canute to claim the throne of England

Canute (Cnut), 1017–1035

To consolidate his position with the Saxons Canute married Emma, the widow of Ethelred II. He began his career in the usual Danish/Norse way with fire, sword and general barbarity, yet afterwards he is reputed to have become a humane and wise monarch. He restored English customs at a general assembly and ensured to the Danes and English equal rights of protection of person and property, even preferring English subjects to important posts. Nevertheless, he remained relentless in his pursuit of further power. First he gained undisputed control of Denmark and then subdued Sweden into a vassal kingdom. In 1028 he conquered Norway and in 1031 invaded Scotland.

He was born about 994 and died in 1035 at Shaftsbury in Dorset, and is buried at Winchester. He was a pragmatic man who, in order to quell the fawning flatterers of his court, chose to demonstrate human fallibility by having his chair placed by the seaside at low tide. When the tide came in with the obvious result he asked them to note that nature ruled supreme. In all he left a memory of a stern but just king.

There is a rather poignant story of the period when Canute, nearly a thousand years ago, lived in the beautiful seaside hamlet of Bosham on the Sussex coast. In that village there is a pretty and lovingly cared-for church, on the floor of which under a commemorative tablet is buried the little daughter of King Canute. She died after falling into the mill race which is still channelled into the sea nearby. During excavations years ago there was also found a skeleton, adjacent to that of the child, which some historians believe to be that of Harold, the last Saxon King. According to chroniclers, the injuries conform to those suffered by Harold at Hastings and they suspect that his body was brought there in secret and not to Waltham Abbey. He too had spent much of his life at Bosham.

Harald, 1035–1040

An indication of Canute's wide-ranging power in Europe during that time lies in the fact that he was able to leave the crown of Norway to his eldest son Sweyn, and England to his second son Harald, who reigned for five years until 1040, dying at the age of 23. Canute left Denmark to his third son Hardicanute.

Hardicanute, 1040–1042

Upon the English throne becoming vacant, Hardicanute returned and reigned as the monarch until 1042 when he died at the early age of 24. With the death of Hardicanute came also the end of the short-lived Danish dynasty, the succession devolving to the Saxon line once more in the form of Edward the Confessor, his maternal brother, who had been living in Normandy to where his mother had retired.

Edward the Confessor, 1042–1066

Edward the Confessor was so called because he was almost constantly at prayer. He died on 5 January 1066 at the age of 63. He was a weak, superstitious but well-intentioned man who gained the affection of the population by his sanctity and his respect for the administration of justice. More of a cleric than a ruler, he paid little heed to the affairs of state and had for many years entrusted the governance of the country to Harold Godwin. He spent most of his time in prayer or engaged in ecclesiastical matters either in England or France. His connections with Normandy were very strong: his mother Emma was Norman and had returned there to live out her retirement. He too had spent part of his childhood there and was living there, spending most of his time in religious contemplation, when the short span of Danish kings consisting of Canute and his two sons Harold I and Hardicanute came to a close. As the son of Ethelred II and stepson of Canute he was brought back from Normandy to occupy the throne. In spite of his attachment to justice, his lack of attention to proper administration caused confusion in regard to the succession. He died childless and had not officially nominated a successor. Clearly this left a situation to be exploited by the ambitious and powerful who could back up their claim to the throne with believable argument as well as an army, and there was one waiting who fulfilled all those conditions – Duke William of Normandy. In Christian countries the Pope played a pivotal role in the selection and establishment of a successor to a vacant throne. His decisions, usually made after long deliberation, were required in cases where there was more than one claimant. It was important to avoid the possibility of leaving grounds for further dispute and/or conflict.

2

The Birth of Normandy and Beyond

The area of France now known as Normandy was invaded by the Vikings (named 'Norsemen' by the French) under a leader named Rollo, during the ninth century. They liked the area and there they settled. After several unsuccessful attempts to dislodge them, the French King Charles III, in 912, officially ceded the land to them and created the Dukedom of Normandy. Henceforth they were referred to as Normans. By giving formal recognition, Charles clearly defined their hierarchical position in the country. In turn, by accepting a dukedom Rollo and his descendants signalled equally clearly their own acceptance of the French king as their overlord. Following their settlement in France, the Normans experienced closer contact with their Christian hosts from whom they not only acquired more social polish but in the process they exchanged paganism for Christianity. By accepting this conversion they automatically subjugated themselves to the jurisdiction of the Pope on certain matters impinging on all sovereigns of Christian countries.

Nevertheless, given the restless aggression which characterized the Normans it was inevitable that they would eventually alienate their neighbours and then extend their domains to take control of vast areas, much in excess of the land originally ceded to them as a fiefdom. This they did, not only by further conquest but sometimes by the more legally acceptable way of acquisition, through influential marriages. By the middle of the eleventh century, under the leadership of William the Bastard (later to become the Conqueror), they controlled Brittany, were spreading south into Maine and had forged an alliance in Flanders, a situation which gave the French an impression of impending encirclement, resulting in growing concern.

That the Normans were now Christian gave rise to the view that it might inhibit Duke William against any attempt to overthrow the French king, who was a bastion of the Catholic religion in Europe – but they could not be sure. Such an action would have had an unstabling effect on the whole continent, probably would not have been sanctioned by the Pope, and might have led to excommunication. To act contrary to such protocol would also have ranged the whole of Christian Europe against William. This left the rapacious leader of Normandy face to face with the bald fact that his ambitions, at least on the Continent, seemed to be limited to a dukedom. For a man like William this in no measure satiated his political appetite. To quench it he obviously had to seek satisfaction elsewhere – but where?

A situation was developing on the other side of the Channel which held out the prospect of meeting his ambitions. It needed much thought and planning to carry through a plan forming in his mind. There were certain factions which would need to be enlisted as allies, or at least nullified as potential antagonists, if he were to bring it to fruition. The prize he had in mind was the throne of England. If he could carry out his plans he might need more than simply the acquiescence of those who may be capable of thwarting them. England had become a powerful military force led by a capable commander in King Harold II. He therefore set about convincing those who might oppose his plans, as well as those who could aid them, of how they would benefit by his success.

A Disputed Succession

Saxons observed the rule of primogeniture in the matter of succession to the throne, but with an important caveat. If circumstances dictated that the candidate was unsuitable, whatever the reason, the selection was conducted on practical grounds by a council called the 'Witan' ('Witangemot'). This council was composed from various aspects of society: the most senior ecclesiastics, members of the extended royal family, earls and a small class of landowners known as the King's Thegns. It was this body which decided upon the appointment of Harold Godwin who, although not of royal lineage, had proved himself a natural and successful leader. He had been running the affairs of state for about 13 years having been thrust into the role by the royal advisers with the consent of Edward the Confessor, who was indifferent to worldly affairs. There being no heir, Godwin no doubt felt entitled to presume that the death of the king would result in his succession to the throne. This was always conditional upon receiving the approval of the Witan. After the death of Edward, the council unhesitatingly approved his nomination and he was crowned. It was believed that it would avoid the chaos which might result from a dynastic vacuum where opportunistic factions may use a prospective contender to promote internal rivalry. It could not, however, obviate those who might decide to stake a claim by force of arms. Harold Hardrada of Norway was one with such thoughts. He was drawn to the prospect and possessed a powerful army. He was also harbouring Harold Godwin's brother Tostig in Scandinavia, using him as a pawn to add respectability to his claim. Tostig had been thrown out of Northumbria by people who were not prepared to suffer any more of his tyranny. Later events showed that Tostig and his ostensible benefactor succumbed to the temptation and took the risk to invade. They chose the north east of England

19

probably because Tostig knew the coastal areas where a landing would be easiest. It is understood that they were inveigled into their decision by William who appeared to be championing their cause. It is doubtful that they were fully cognisant of the scope of William's intentions or preparations for invasion.

Another claimant was the grandson of Edmund Ironside, known as Edward the Atheling, who, with his family, had been in exile in Hungary from whence they returned, probably about 1057. When their safety was assured he went with his sister Margaret to Scotland where she married Malcolm III. Despite a suggestion that Edward did at one time favour Atheling's claim, he was obviously disregarded by both the Witan and Harold.

Upon the death of Edward the Confessor, William the Bastard, Duke of Normandy, stated that he had so convincing a claim that it rendered all others invalid. First, he recounted that in 1051 Harold had been shipwrecked near the coast of France and was taken to William's castle and for a period held in virtual captivity there. During that time William maintained that he had secured from Harold a promise to support his claim to the throne when Edward died. One can reasonably assume that if such a demand was made of Harold while he was incarcerated in Falaise Castle, it would have been a prudent move on his part to agree with his host, otherwise the outcome would certainly have had fatal consequences. It is open to conjecture whether under duress this might have happened. The only circumstantial evidence is that Harold was allowed to return to England, which could suggest that the claim was not without foundation. The opinion of most would probably incline to the view that, even if true, the method employed to extract such a pledge would render it invalid.

According to the *Anglo-Saxon Chronicle*, late in the year 1051 William the Bastard, with members of his court, visited

Edward the Confessor in England. In the course of the meeting, he claimed, Edward promised the crown of England to him when the time came. Bearing in mind the traditional function of the Witan with regard to matters relating to the succession, this claim appears to be somewhat fragile. At the time, Edward was about 48 and did not engage in warlike pursuits liable to cut short his life. This reduced the risks to his health considerably. One wonders why such a subject would arise at a social event. Edward would also have been fully cognisant of the rights and formalities in the selection of a king. He was a man reputed to be an ardent seeker of justice, which alone would have inhibited him from ignoring the rights of the Witan in the whole process: it was not within the gift of any king to be sole broker in the matter. Added to this was the fact that William was only about 24 at the time. All of this throws a shadow over William's version of events.

William considered that the promises, which he alleged had been made to him, constituted sufficient legal grounds to lay his claim before the Pope. He fortified his case by promising the Pope that should he be successful he would build two magnificent churches in France. After the conquest he fulfilled his promise by building La St Trinite (Church of the Abbaye-aux-Dames) and St Etienne (Church of the Abbaye aux Hommes) in Caen. He was buried in the latter.

Other factors which weighed in William's favour in terms of receiving papal blessing to grasp the throne of England were of a more insidious nature, because of his potential to menace the peace and stability of the French throne. The Church had been instrumental in setting up the current French royal family and in turn relied heavily upon them to sustain and further the cause of the Roman Church in Europe. William did not acknowledge the rights of the Church to hold sway over every aspect of secular life, but tended to concede only whenever necessary in order to gain an advantage in other areas.

In the meantime, matters concerning territorial incursion and possession had taken a dangerous turn in the struggle between Geoffrey Martel of Anjou and the Duke of Normandy. The king of France at that time did not directly control much of the country in his own right, but relied on alliances with powerful baronial leaders such as Martel, whose side he had taken in the conflict. Their joint forces were defeated by William on the battlefields of Mortemer and Varaville 1054 and 1058 respectively. This constituted a transfer in the balance of power in France and from it arose the possibility that this ambitious, rapacious and cruel Norman leader may even be capable of defying the established order. The risks, both regal and papal, were considerable should he decide to risk all and take his ambitions further, overthrow the French king, and don the French crown himself.

It must have crossed their minds that the ultimate diversion lay in the hands of the papal authority. Agreement for William to invade England held out certain possibilities that might solve other vexing problems troubling the French monarchy as well as the Pope. William might be defeated and killed which would remove him from the scene in France and possibly enable the king and the Pope to ennoble a successor in Normandy who would probably be 'their man', and therefore more emollient – plus, Normandy might also be regained for France, by default. If, on the other hand, William won, he would still be bound by his promises of allegiance and to the building of great churches in France, for the greater glory of Rome, and might be persuaded to continue a similar programme in England. More importantly, he would thenceforth be preoccupied with establishing himself in England and as a consequence would be removed as an immediate threat to French regal security. It would have been most unusual for these aspects not to have come under some scrutiny by the major parties concerned.

The painstaking plotting and conniving of William the

Bastard indeed came to fruition when permission to usurp the throne of England by violent means was granted and he was able to embark on his conspiracy with Hardrada and Tostig. England at that time was considered to be the best governed and one of the most prosperous countries in Europe. The aftermath of the invasion was one of extreme carnage and pillage. In an age when violence was commonplace the scale of the excesses perpetrated by William's army appalled other European rulers. Even more astonishing was the fact that the man who gave permission for William to undertake this mission was none other than the highest authority in the Christian world at the time, Pope Gregory VII. He obviously totally misread the true nature and character of the man with whom he had been dealing. This must be the answer because no one could imagine a true soldier capable of such atrocities against a civilian population.

One could speculate that there might have been a motive of deeper significance attached to William's overall strategy. We know he was not a forgiving man and at the back of his mind he may have had a historical grudge against the Norwegian Royal House. In 863, Harold (or Harald) I (Haarfager – 'Beautiful hair'), one of the greatest monarchs in Norwegian history, succeeded his father to the throne. He brought all the Norwegian *jarls* under his control until the whole of the country was subject to his rule. This 20-year war of attrition was brought to a close in 885. At the outset of the war he declared he would not have his hair cut until he had achieved his mission, hence the soubriquet. The conquered *jarls* emigrated to Iceland, Shetland, the Orkneys and the Faroes. Another named Rollo (or Hrolf), took his followers westwards and they settled in a place which came to be named Normandy.

3

An Invasion Begins

The large Scandinavian army landed on the north-east coast on 25 September 1066 and then proceeded to march on York. According to all accounts it was greater than any of its predecessors and within days had destroyed the northern army at the battle of Fulford.

Harold was at that time guarding the south coast against an impending invasion from Normandy, but upon hearing of the attack in the north he led his army in a forced march to confront the Norsemen.

Within 10 days his army had reached York, a formidable achievement. He immediately launched an assault on the Scandinavians at a place called Stamford Bridge about seven miles from York. It was a long and bloody battle which resulted in the destruction of about 90 per cent of the invading force.

An indication of the scale of the losses sustained by the Norse army in the battle is reflected by the fact that at least 300 ships were needed to bring them to England, but after the survivors had negotiated a truce it required a mere 23 to transport them back home.

Nevertheless, in the winning of such a conflict, Harold's army had sustained extensive losses in dead and wounded. Coming on top of the rapid march north undoubtedly all of them would have suffered from severe exhaustion. Normally a considerable period of respite would have been required to allow the army to recover. Unfortunately, this was not to be available to them because within three days Harold learned that William had landed a large invasion force at Pevensey Bay on the south coast.

To counter this new threat the remnants of his army would be required to undertake another forced march of about 250 miles. Fatefully, by the time this news arrived he had already given permission to those of his troops who had requested leave of absence to return to their farms or smallholdings to prepare for the onset of winter. In those times, failure to make adequate provision for food against the winter months meant that families were unlikely to survive.

Hastings

The depleted and tired force that eventually took the field at a place later named Battle, a few miles north of Hastings, on 14 October 1066, against a formidable enemy which was well fed, rested and embedded in positions of strength, was in no condition to prevail against such an adversary. The battle of Stamford Bridge had without question played a major part in determining the outcome of the meeting between the Norman army and the remnants of that which Harold was able to muster. William must have been jubilant that the timing of Stamford Bridge dovetailed so beautifully with his own plans. The weather also seemed to have conspired to make the transportation of a large army across the Channel so much easier. Further consolation lay in that enough damage had already been inflicted on Harold's army to swing the balance of success in William's favour. The strategy cunningly devised by William had undoubtedly worked.

The outcome was a defeat for Saxon England and marked a turning point in English history. Then followed fundamental changes in laws and social organization. Continental feudalism removed many long-held freedoms. It heralded the commencement of a regime which was every bit as bad as the ravages of the Vikings over a century earlier, the difference being that instead of pagan savages the Normans were supposed to be civilised Christians.

The Occupation

England did not automatically become a Norman possession at a stroke but had to be conquered gradually. Naturally there was resistance everywhere as the population realised the gravity of the situation, but as the country was now leaderless these isolated uprisings were quickly snuffed out. In a swift but carefully orchestrated programme the genius and forethought of the Normans was clearly demonstrated by the fact that as they conquered each particular area they immediately built a castle. The first were of the motte and bailey type which consisted of a large mound or hill on top of which was built a simple fortification. From the comparative safety of the castle a small body of marauding cavalry could make sporadic raids to terrorize the inhabitants of the area and plunder their livestock and food supplies. The archers remained behind to defend the castle walls. If the resistance encountered locally by the cavalry was too great they retired behind their defences until the local uprising petered out. They then resumed their demoralising raids until the relentlessness of their tactics forced the local peasantry to accept them as rulers. Paradoxically it was like a reversal, or distortion, of modern-day guerrilla tactics. Whereas in modern times guerrilla movements rely on secrecy, anonymity and surprise tactics, the Normans remained an obvious but permanent threat, secure behind their unassailable castle walls. This technique was so effective that within five years they had built no fewer than 31 such castles, ranging as far apart as Dover in the south east to Monmouth on the Welsh border and as far to the north and north east as Chester and York. Even so, dogged resistance continued for years. The brave resistance by the Welsh led the Normans to build castles in almost every corner of Wales. Gwent, Chepstow, Monmouth, Gower, Cardigan, Radnor, Brecknock, the Vale of Clywdd and Montgomeryshire were selected to subdue and dominate the population. In the twelfth century they also settled Pembrokeshire with so many English and Flemish farmers that it became known as 'little England'.

Part of the army of William I consisted of skilled Breton archers. The Bretons were close cousins of the Welsh and their language was equally closely related. By a twist of fate, the Bretons, whose expert archers played such a crucial part in the success of the Normans at Hastings, helped to lay the foundations for the later brutal subjugation of Wales.

However, a rebellious spirit existed within the breast of a small Lincolnshire farmer named Hereward (the Wake) who, dispossessed of his land, led his band of guerrilla fighters in spirited resistance in the Fen country until in 1071 a major campaign was mounted against him by William on both land and sea until he was finally defeated.

The fiercest resistance of all came from the north: Yorkshire, Westmorland, Cumberland and particularly Northumbria/ Bernicia, which extended from the Humber up to the Firth of Forth including Edinburgh. There culminated a series of coordinated attacks by William's main forces which were not merely designed to put down a revolt as to almost annihilate the population and destroy their way of life. This was accomplished to such a degree that 21 years later, when William the Conqueror had the *Domesday Book* prepared, the effects of the devastation were still so evident that the region was not considered worth including in the survey. The chilling evidence of this is that the entry against the area was categorised by one word: 'WASTE'. Many fled to Scotland and no doubt took with them their fear and hatred of the new Norman regime. The treatment by William I of this part of England, after laying it waste, was tantamount to discarding it from the realm, leaving it as a devastated and ungoverned region. The return of previous occupants of the farmsteads was inevitable, once they sensed that there was an opportunity, however hard the task, to resume their lives. At least now that the Normans held the area in such little regard they might anticipate relative peace from that direction. Thus the Lothians, particularly, at that time would have been thrust into a sort of political limbo. The abominable devastation by William extending throughout Yorkshire in the south left them somewhat isolated and thereby reduced their ability to defend themselves as a unified group.

The Northumbrian Angles and Saxons had founded a well populated agrarian society throughout the south of what is now Scotland. Their King Edwin was the founder of Edinburgh. The region was then known as Bernicia. The immutable evidence of their number is still seen to this day in the overwhelming variety of names of English origin. Their language was Old English, in common with those of the south, from whom they had become separated through William's brutal subjugation of the area. To the north there was the region occupied by the Scots who had invaded from Ireland and, having wiped the Picts from history, were now firmly established as kings of Caledonia, at that time under Malcolm III (Canmore). From his seat in Perthshire he would have been fully aware of events in the south, the resistance to the Normans followed by the devastation resulting in the isolation of those Nothumbrians north of the Tweed, leaving them vulnerable. Danger could come from raiding Vikings or from his own army. The situation was ripe for exploitation from Canmore's point of view. In the first place they were obviously unprepared to withstand an attack by his forces, and in addition they had no prospect of acquiring a strong ally. He was ambitious to extend his kingdom and here was presented with a perfect opportunity. It is my firm belief that rather than attack them and destroy a fruitful area he offered them an alliance under his kingship. In doing this he gained in every manner, bloodlessly obtaining additional territory together with numerous new subjects beholden to him for their future protection. It follows that had he eliminated them then both the place and occupational names of the countryside would have gone with them as well, and been replaced with those of Celtic usage; presumably the English language would also have been replaced by Gaelic.

Malcolm had spent some time at the English court before the conquest and, following the death of his first wife, married Margaret, a granddaughter of Edward Ironside, an earlier Saxon king. This highly educated and refined English lady was probably the most influential woman in Scottish history. She was responsible for many reforms in the Scottish Church and also brought about many changes in Scottish social life. Her extraordinary work on behalf of both was recognised by the Scots in 1290 when she was sanctified. A chapel dedicated to her memory can be found in Edinburgh Castle.

Observing the hostility generated by William's brutality, Malcolm decided that it would now be an opportune moment to annexe the most northerly, and largely undefended, parts of this now ravaged region, but with its fertile lands remaining. He invaded in 1070 but his invasion was punished by a punitive force sent by William I. Undeterred he ventured again and further into Northumberland. On this occasion William decided that he should be tamed and invaded Scotland in 1072. He completely defeated Malcolm, but to drive the point home he pursued him as far as the Tay where he made him swear fealty to him as his overlord. Malcolm was also forced to hand over his son Duncan as a hostage

It probably became clear to William that although he had

conquered Scotland militarily, there were two inherent impediments which would prevent him holding it in an uncontested state without creating a dependable method of governorship. One was the geography which made regular winter campaigns almost impossible and the other was his vast and continuing commitments in France, where not only Normandy but also the other provinces under his control, such as Anjou and Brittany, were under regular attack. All this was in addition to the ardent desire of the French monarchy to be rid of him from within the borders of France entirely. To this end, they were actively fomenting unrest in the provinces under his dominion.

William believed the solution lay in retaining Malcolm as a subordinate king. The uncertainty of this arrangement was underlined when, after the departure of William to the south, Malcolm broke the treaty and continued to invade northern England, ravaging the countryside and enslaving or killing its people. He outlived William the Conqueror but was himself killed in battle, at Alnwick, by forces under William II (Rufus), during another attempted invasion of England in 1093.

After the deaths of his father and brothers, David I succeeded to the throne of Scotland. He immediately raised an army to invade England and was comprehensively defeated at the Battle of the Standard in 1138. It would appear that David suspected that it might only be a matter of time before the presence of the Normans in the Lothians and elsewhere in Scotland would offer a threat to him which could conceivably usurp his sovereignty. He had spent much of his youth at the English court, was an admirer of the method of administration evolved by the Norman rulers in England, and wished to introduce it into Scotland. The system was a combination of the English shire system with its sheriff or reeve and borough courts, reinforced by the strict Norman feudal system. David embarked upon a deliberate policy whereby he actively encouraged more Norman nobility to come to Scotland by inviting them to take over large grants of land. This continued until, apart from the western highlands and islands, the Normans became the ruling aristocracy of Scotland. An important factor from the point of view of David was that this hegemony of military elite was then bound to him, as benefactor and leader.

This is an interesting period in the affairs of England and Scotland and gives some clues as to how the border between the two countries might possibly have changed and finally evolved. One of the Norman knights who fought on the side of William at Hastings was, as a reward, afterwards given large tracts of land in Yorkshire and the north of England together with the office of Earl of the Lothians and Cumbria. In maintaining the security of the borders from Edinburgh to below Carlisle he engaged frequently in hostilities against the Scots. One of his descendants, of the same name, was destined to play a more significant part in the affairs of both countries in a totally different context. His name was Robert de Brus (Bruce). His father, Robert, Earl of Carrick, had been a staunch supporter of England and had accompanied Edward I to Palestine in 1269.

The fortunes of the de Brus family were increased still further by David I when he granted them lands in the south west of Scotland. This was an area which had not been previously occupied by the Saxons. It meant that on both sides of the border the de Brus family were now an immensely powerful force and in some ways could be seen almost as intermediaries between the two courts. There is no doubt that these were the beginnings of a journey which took them to the throne of Scotland and from which they led the drive to achieve Scotland's independence.

David acquired a considerable reputation for sanctity which was no doubt well deserved, but a study of his actions suggests a man who was more far-sighted and worldly than many suspected. When he decided to build abbeys at Holyrood, Melrose, Jedburgh, Kelso, Dryburgh and Newbattle, he was fully aware that they were located within the Lothians, which was still English territory overseen by the Bruce family. He may have calculated that because of the religious nature of his enterprise it would be extremely difficult for the English monarchy to gainsay such actions. It would also have occurred to him that the absence of such objections on territorial grounds would have far-reaching consequences. The users of these edifices and religious houses would be (although ostensibly open to all) invariably those dwelling in the locality. Once built they became not only part of the ecclesiastical life of the region but over time identified with the king, who inaugurated them and accepted them, along with the territory, as coming under his jurisdiction. Whether this was a calculated plan or not, it effectively gave impetus to the transfer of the Lothians to Scotland. Previously, periodic battles or assumptions of ownership had made only temporary alterations to the boundary, whereas this change embodied permanency. In many ways it was a masterclass in diplomacy.

It is a Scottish boast that, unlike the English, they were never conquered by the Normans. This claim is refuted by the events at Abernethy in 1072 when William forced Malcolm to acknowledge his overlordship and surrender his son as hostage. If this is not acknowledged as a victory, the English would claim that by the actions of David I, the Scots gradually gave away their country to the Normans without putting up a fight. Considering the warlike nature of Scottish society at the time, this would seem unlikely. Another incontrovertible fact is that had they not been in thrall to successive rulers including the Normans, the fight for Scottish independence by the Norman leaders of Scotland almost 250 years later would have been unnecessary.

Whatever version may be agreed, the fact remains that the Normans, from the end of the eleventh century onwards, dominated almost every aspect of life in Britain, even to the point of, in 1314, establishing themselves as kings of Scotland. From the ascent of the de Brus family to the throne, right through to the Stuarts, every Scottish king was of Norman origin. The name of Stewart, which later became Stuart, was a corruption of the title of the bearer of the office of 'steward' to the Scottish king, in fact an occupational name. The real family name of this group was 'Fitzalan', and they were of Breton origin. From their post-conquest base in Shropshire they too moved to Scotland and thence into the office of Grand 'Steward' of Scotland from which they eventually took their name.

Taking the succession even further, through intermarriage between the Fitzalans and Bruce families, the Stewarts succeeded to the crown of Scotland. The marriage of James IV of Scotland to Margaret Tudor of England provided the necessary connection to the English throne which, after the death of Elizabeth I culminated in the union of the crowns of England and Scotland.

This was the point when the Stuarts began to a claim connection with divinity. They declared that they enjoyed 'the divine right of kings' which made them the representatives of God in monarchical form. From their origins as Shropshire barons, this was quite a step.

Castles

The use of castles was vital to William in order to consolidate his victory at Hastings. The first were of the motte and bailey design which was a large earth mound topped by a simple castle. The English did not fortify their settlements in this way but it was common in Normandy for the population to be governed from a

---

series of carefully located castles, providing the soldiers with a secure defensive stronghold from which to control the local area. William was no mean exponent in the art of designing and building all manner of edifices, and castles, cathedrals, churches and abbeys would have come under his scrutiny in Normandy. It is recorded that when he landed at Pevensey Bay he brought with him a prefabricated wooden fort. In this he set up his first headquarters, siting it within the existing and extensive walls of a Roman castle for greater security.

The first really strong castle was situated at Dover where there had previously been a fairly basic one, the foundations of which were employed to erect a much more substantial structure. As early as AD 1071 castles had been constructed at the following places:

- Berkeley
- Cambridge
- Chepstow
- Chester
- Clifford
- Dover
- Ewyas Harold
- Exeter
- Hastings
- Hereford
- Huntingdon
- Lincoln
- London (2)
- Monmouth
- Montacute
- Oxford
- Pevensey
- Shrewsbury

- Stafford
- WallinfordWarwick
- Wigmore
- Winchester
- Wisbech
- Worcester
- York (2)

Ewyas Harold was a pre-Norman castle built with permission of Edward the Confessor who gave preferment to some of his Norman cronies whom he had invited into England. They were much resented by the local population because of their offensive attitude.

Some castles still remain intact, others are ruins, and some have disappeared altogether, but all are worth locating if only to gain an impression of their part in history and the development of the town where each is, or was, sited. A superb book to consult on castles is that by Paul Johnson in cooperation with the English National Trust. It takes the reader back to the Iron Age with fascinating and imaginative information.

The New Dynasty

William the Conqueror, Duke of Normandy, 1066–1087

William was the illegitimate son of Robert 'the Devil', Duke of Normandy and Arletta, who died suddenly while returning from a pilgrimage to Jerusalem when William was only 8. To inherit the dukedom of Normandy at such a vulnerable age placed William in a hazardous position. The fact that he survived to maturity and took over the succession speaks volumes for those who acted as his guardians. After all, he was not legitimate and his father had a legitimate son, which meant William must have been used as some kind of political pawn to accommodate another party.

Whatever the explanation, he reached an age and possessed the ability to take control of probably the largest principality in Europe at the time. Constant challenges to his position from rebellious nobles were having to be repulsed, and as a result he became a formidable warrior and leader. The last of these was crushed in the battle of Val des Dunes in 1047. This confirmed his absolute control of Normandy. After his accession to the English throne he had an even greater army to call upon, which would deter further military challenges from individual sources.

In 1087 William was still warring with the French, who resented his retention of Normandy and other French possessions in addition to the crown of England. Their hopes that he would relinquish them, and be out of their hair once he had gained England, were cruelly dashed. To be rid of him they began to suborn his Normandy-based nobles. The result was that a number of rebellions broke out against him. Reacting in the time-honoured way he led an army against them and committed a series of atrocities. He was engaged in reducing the town of Mantes to burnt rubble when, with poetic justice, his horse stumbled on a hot timber. He was thrown violently against the pommel of his saddle. Serious internal injuries resulted, from which he died. His body was then taken to the Abbey of St Gervais. Upon his death it was seen that when matters such as a settled succession to the throne arose he was no better than Edward the Confessor. The instructions he left gave little hope for a peaceful resolution, especially so because his sons were men who had been brought up in an atmosphere of violence, paying scant regard to diplomatic practices, with all disputes being settled by force of arms.

At least one of these violent men was incited to express

his emotions to the full when he discovered that William had ignored the accepted right of primogeniture. Instead of naming his eldest son Robert Curthose (so called because of his short legs) to inherit the crown, he chose to designate him Duke of Normandy and to bequeath the English crown to William (Rufus), his second-born. In doing so he sowed the seeds of serious discord, igniting sibling rivalry between these volatile characters. Continuous rebellions and risings resulted. Although Robert and William Rufus eventually made peace, for a time there were serious clashes. Following their reconciliation they combined to fight against Welsh and Scots in various actions.

William II (Rufus), 1087–1100

William II was another warrior king, stern and avaricious, unjust and unpopular. He quarrelled with his own appointee Anselm, Archbishop of Canterbury, over the right to the ownership of Church property and finally drove him into exile. After the death of William I, Malcolm III of Scotland invaded again but in 1093 he was defeated by Rufus and killed at Alnwick, Northumbria.

Rufus, like most royalty, was an enthusiastic hunter and it was on one of these excursions in the New Forest in 1100 that he met his death. He was shot by an arrow (accidentally or otherwise) discharged from the bow of a French gentleman named Walter Tyrell, or Tirel. Although claiming his innocence Tyrell decided that his best defence was absence and fled to Normandy. Personally unloved by the bulk of his subjects someone obviously mourned Rufus's passing because the alleged site of his death is marked by the 'Rufus Stone', located in the New Forest just off the A31 a few miles west of Cadnam in Hampshire. His only redeeming moment seems to have been the building of the Westminster Hall, completed in 1097, later famous as being the meeting place of the first parliamentary session in 1264 during the rule of Henry III. The Hall was rebuilt between 1397 and 1399 during the reign of Richard II on the same foundations.

HENRY I ('Beauclerc' or 'fine scholar'), 1100–1135

Coincidentally, if you are willing to believe it, Henry (the fourth son of the Conqueror), and the brother of William Rufus, had been hunting in the same locality and on the same day as the 'accident' suffered by his brother. On hearing the news he disregarded any niceties or respect which might have been due to his brother and proceeded immediately to Winchester to secure the treasury and institute proceedings for his own coronation, which took place only three days later. An educated man, he instituted or restored laws and overhauled the justice system. He also initiated a fairer taxation method. These measures earned him the title 'The Lion of Justice'. Significantly, Tyrell returned to England at this time and seemed to have been held in high regard by the king, and even rewarded. No doubt that confirmed earlier speculation by some! As expected, the dissatisfaction of his older brother Robert boiled up. He had once again been passed over as heir to the throne. He and his brother Henry met to settle their differences by force of arms at a place called Tinchebrai in Normandy in 1106. Once again Robert Curthose, one might say, came up short. He was defeated, taken prisoner and spent the next 28 years, until his death, incarcerated in Cardiff Castle. Henry I was obviously not a man unduly hindered by warm fraternal feelings. Thanks to the defeat of his brother at Tinchebrai he acquired the lands of Normandy previously bequeathed to Robert by his father, thenceforth dividing his time between this rich province and his court in England.

Although Henry had fathered a large number of illegitimate children he had only two from within marriage: a son, William, and a daughter, Matilda. Had all gone to plan his son would have succeeded him to the throne but in 1120 the 'White Ship', in which the young man was crossing the Channel, sank leaving no survivors. There was now no male heir and another disputed succession was created. It is recorded that all those aboard the ship had imbibed too liberally, a practice not recommended as a concomitant to good seamanship. Some years before he died, Henry, after a great struggle, forced his nobles, including his nephew Stephen, and Church elders to accept the nomination of his daughter Matilda as heir to the throne, but after his death the agreement was declared invalid on the grounds that he had extracted it under duress. The ruling class rejected her claim and chose instead Henry's nephew Stephen, though his claim was the weaker. The fact is that they did not want a female on the throne.

Geoffrey, Archbishop of Monmouth (later Archbishop of St Asaph, 1152)

This was the era of Norman settlement in South Wales. In 1139, Geoffrey of Monmouth, a historian and ecclesiastic, on hearing some of the myths and legends abounding in the area, wrote a book entitled *History of the Britons* (*Historia Britonum*), an apocryphal account of kings of Britain dating from Brut, the supposed first king, through to Cadwallader in the seventh century. One of the kings was likened to Arthur, extolling his victories over Saxons and Picts. Although it was entirely a work of fiction, the writer claimed it as being based on an ancient book written in the Breton language which had been discovered by a fellow archbishop. It gained considerable popularity as a romance and was translated into various languages.

Contested succession

As noted above, the two claimants for the throne following the death of Henry I were cousins, both grandchildren of William the Conqueror: Stephen of Blois and Matilda. The line was thus: Adela, daughter of William the Conqueror, married Stephen, Count of Blois. Their son, also named Stephen, thrust himself forward as the obvious successor immediately the death of Henry I was announced. There was an older son but he was a bishop and stood aside in favour of Stephen, who assumed the throne amidst controversy. The first part of his claim rested on being the grandson of William the Conqueror. In addition, he was male, and under Salic Law took precedence. This was in direct contradiction of the oath he had given, in the company of others, that he would honour the wishes of Henry to uphold the succession of Matilda.

Stephen did not wait to engage in the formalities of debate. In defiance of Matilda's claim he moved in quickly to seize the crown. In taking it he received support from his brother Henry, the Bishop of Winchester, who in turn procured for him an endorsement of his claim from Pope Innocent II. This carried great influence with the general populace. His character was weak and insecure, totally lacking in the decisive qualities essential in a king during those turbulent times. Impossible to disguise, these traits were soon frustratingly clear to the barons. In 1139, when the Empress Matilda landed in England, the civil war that followed was labelled the 'Anarchy'. The same barons were now resorting to tyrannical and destructive behaviour in defiance of the laws of the land. The scribes of the time lamented that 'Christ and the Saints slept'. The period was described as being 'nineteen bitter winters'.

Matilda was first married, at the age of 13, to the German emperor, Henry V, who died in 1125 at the age of about 44. (Interestingly, the king betrothed her to the German prince when she was only 8 years old, whereupon she went to Germany to be educated – a move no doubt calculated to cement an alliance). After becoming a widow at the age of 22 she was then married off to Geoffrey IV, Count of Anjou, who was the head of one of the most powerful families in France, thereby forging another strong alliance. Even after her re-marriage this very strong-willed woman insisted on retaining the title of 'empress'.

Matilda was adamant that, as the daughter of Henry I, she was of closer kin because she had descended through the male line. She insisted her claim was reinforced by the nomination made by her father. The barons argued that this was only achieved by coercion. However, she was not without allies. One was her uncle David I of Scotland. Ostensibly in her support he invaded the north of England. His purpose was not just to take up her cause but to try to profit by the confusion reigning at the time and annexe Northumbria to Scotland. At the Battle of the Standard which took place near Northallerton in Yorkshire on 22 August 1138, the Scots under David suffered a comprehensive defeat. The battle derived its name from the fact that the English levies fought under the banners of St Cuthbert, St Wilfred and St John of Beverley. Matilda first tried diplomatic measures to pursue her demands. When this failed, she began to garner military support for her cause abroad.

Before committing herself to action she also secured substantial support in England itself and ingratiated herself with the Church. When her army was ready she entered England in 1139. In this she received help from her bastard half-brother Robert of Gloucester who was a formidable soldier. A series of opening exchanges led eventually to a pitched battle at Lincoln in 1142, during which Stephen was taken prisoner. He was released in exchange for Matilda's half-brother Robert, who had been captured by Stephen's forces. Sporadic conflict between the parties continued over a long period. Matilda had in the meantime gained control of London. The citizens welcomed her initially but found her arrogant behaviour unbearable and drove her out. About the same time, Robert died, leaving her without a military leader on whom she could rely.

The war reached a critical point in 1142 when Matilda was besieged in Oxford Castle, but she managed to escape across the frozen Thames after which she passed control of the army to her son, Henry of Anjou. He mustered his forces both in Normandy and England and mounted an invasion in 1149 which Stephen repulsed. His second attempt in 1153 finally resulted in agreement between the warring factions. Conditions arose which removed the motivation for Stephen to continue. His son and heir, Eustace, died and he himself was suffering failing health. Through the Treaty of Wallingford in 1153 peace and stability were re-established on the understanding that Stephen would remain king for the remainder of his life but be succeeded by Henry of Anjou when the time came.

It came sooner than Henry expected. Less than a year later the king was dead. He died at Dover Castle and was interred at Faversham Abbey in 1154. Henry was then crowned Henry II, the first Plantagenet or Angevin king.

A Norman Epilogue

By 1154, in spite of their military might and the iron rule they had imposed, the Norman dynasty in England came to a close, having lasted less than 100 years.

The English might ask whether or not, in an overall sense, their occupation had changed England for the better or worse. The eventual loss of the Lothians certainly reduced the size of England considerably from that held before the Conquest.

There is no clear definitive way of calculating the benefits or detriments – it comes down for the most part to conjecture. From a national security point of view, prior to the Norman invasion the principal danger had always emanated from Scandinavia and this was quashed by Harold in 1066 when he destroyed their vast army at Stamford Bridge. Before that, England was largely a prosperous, peaceful and well governed country content with its borders and under its Wessex kings had become a unified nation. Afterwards it may be claimed, by unifying England and Normandy, command of both shores of the Channel were secured – but to what purpose? Before 1066 we already enjoyed cordial relations including family ties with Normandy. It has been said that through the Norman connection we acquired greater opportunities to establish closer contact with some European countries in some ways more culturally advanced than our own. The argument that this was a new path to enlightenment does not stand up to close scrutiny however. Movement and contact between England and the Continent was commonplace. We have only to look at the reign of Offa, the Mercian King in the latter part of the eighth century, who in concert with Charlemagne, the Frankish emperor, took positive measures to promote trade and learning. Clear evidence shows that 300 years before the Norman invasion people on the Continent benefited from Anglo-Saxon culture and learning. In 782, the great Frankish ruler Charlemagne, while on a visit to Parma in Italy, met Alcuin, the English scholar, and was so impressed by him that he invited him to his court in Tours for the purpose of using his talents in the education of his subjects. To persuade him to stay he established a school, the 'Schola Palatina'. Alcuin, known as 'Flaccus Albinus', was responsible for either founding or improving most of the schools in France as well as building the school in the Abbey of St Martin of Tours. This contact continued in other forms, such as pilgrimage, undertaken as part of the Christian ethic. A hundred years later, Alfred the Great was taken by his father to Rome. Later in his life he incorporated his Christian attitude into the role of kingship. This does not reflect a country starved of erudite contact.

To their credit, the Normans were magnificent builders of churches and cathedrals, but they drew on the craftsmanship of other countries for their achievements. Apart from that, their fame rested primarily on being aggressive warriors and the French, their unwilling hosts, held the Normans of the time in fairly low esteem, deeming them rustic boors who had few manners and spoke poor French. The relatively short-lived Norman annexation of England appeared to have no other purpose than the pursuit of power for its own sake. Ironically the separate Norman identity was lost on the other side of the Channel too, as they were gradually absorbed by the French.

When they first arrived in France they had to learn the language of their new hosts. More than 200 years afterwards they had completely lost their original tongue. When they came to England they brought their version of French with them. They and their successors spent the next 300 years in a futile attempt to make the English use this alien language. Admittedly a substantial number of French words were co-opted into English, and also entered our legal system.

4

The Plantagenet Kings

Henry II

Prior to receiving the crown of England, Henry II became Duke of Normandy. His French possessions also included Anjou, Maine, Touraine and Brittany – in effect an area greater than that ruled by the French King Louis VII. Nevertheless, his possessions in France were held under the terms of feudal law, and therefore, despite holding them, he was still legally a vassal of the French king.

Stephen, by agreement, was still occupying the throne of England when Henry was granted Normandy by his mother Matilda. In the natural course of events Henry had to fulfil his feudal duty and pay homage to the French king. Louis was an ascetic, and some historians have likened him to Edward the Confessor in his devotion to religious worship to the extent that he practically eschewed all worldly pleasures. By a quirk of fate he had been allied to a wife, Eleanor of Aquitaine, whose character and appetites were entirely the opposite to those of her husband.

The man who came to offer his vassalian respects to Louis VII was of a vastly different make-up. Henry was a handsome, young and powerfully-built warrior figure with all the confidence that victories in the field of honour can bestow. The certain prospect of ascending the English throne, linked with his vast estates in France, added to his status. With Louis, to greet Henry, was his beautiful wife Queen Eleanor. Subsequent actions would indicate clearly that there was an instant communion of emotions between the young Henry and the highly attractive but emotionally unfulfilled queen. She was heard to complain that because of her husband's pious and unemotional nature she thought she might have inadvertently married a priest. Obviously, because of their mutual attraction, matters between them were taken further. Some time later she petitioned the Pope to give his sanction to a divorce from Louis on the grounds of consanguinity and its effects on a proper marriage relationship. This was granted in 1152. The royal houses of Europe were aghast when only two months afterwards she and Henry were married. That she had left the French king only to marry the English sovereign was food enough for gossip and all kinds of conjecture, but under the rules of the period she was able to transport with her the rights to her inherited territories in south-west France. Together they ruled the territories of England, Normandy, Brittany, Maine, Anjou, Touraine, Poitou, Guienne and Aquitaine, only ending at the border with Spain.

Bear in mind that when Henry II ascended the throne of England in 1154, he was a mere 21 years of age. With all these vast domains to absorb his attention it was fortunate that he was endowed with a genius for organisation and equally gifted with enormous energy. Such a large territory, so suddenly acquired, coupled with a throne embroiled in anarchy and civil strife would need every ounce. His energetic approach to life is confirmed by the fact that in addition to siring five sons and three daughters legitimately, he had another 20 on the outside of the blanket; the latter being a source of discontent to his wife Eleanor, who wreaked her revenge by eventually turning his sons against him.

Henry instantly set about taming the unruly barons of

England, forcing them to demolish castles which had been built without royal permission. Those who made incursions into England during the reign of Stephen were instantly attacked – for example, William the Lion, the Scottish king who had entered Northumbria once more. The Scottish army was utterly defeated. William was taken prisoner and held in England, not to be released until after the death of Henry.

Henry recognised that it was imperative for agriculture to be revitalised. The havoc caused by Stephen's loss of control over the baronial classes and their general destructiveness had thoroughly ravaged the countryside. Both crop farming and stock production were in dire straits and required concentrated effort to remedy the situation. Part of his plan was to allow landowners to exempt themselves from military service by payment of what was termed 'scutage'. The word derives from the Latin '*scutum*', meaning a knight's shield. In modern times it is used in the expression 'scut free', denoting freed from an obligation. There is another explanation given for this expression which renders it as 'skot free'. This is from the Norwegian and Icelandic word '*skot*', which means a tax. That they sound so similar is immaterial because they also carry a similar meaning.

Henry II was happy to release knights from military duty under this system because it enabled him to use the cash to employ mercenaries. The use of mercenaries was of manifold benefit. They were always available and under his direct control instead of being seconded from the barons. If the barons gave further trouble he had a force constantly under arms with which to discipline them.

The Saxon system of shire courts was revived, incorporating sheriffs, a judge and 12 local men to act as a jury. Over time this replaced the barbarous method of trials by ordeal or battle. Trial by ordeal required that the accused either plunge his hand into boiling liquid or be forced to carry red-hot metal. The speed with which his injuries healed determined his guilt or innocence. Naturally, if he died, the case against him was considered proven. If he survived he was believed to be innocent.

Due to his respect for law and order and the application of forms of justice with which the people felt comfortable, Henry was highly regarded. However, before and even after his marriage to Eleanor, he was a libertine and a wild spirit. In this he was joined by a close friend, Thomas à Becket, who shared the same appetites. Little is known of Becket before this except that he was the son of a wealthy London merchant. Educated at Oxford he was said to have been clever, lighthearted and brave. He had taken part in several battles in France and on one occasion defeated a French knight in single combat. Born circa 1118, his disposition was inclined to pomp and extravagance – he was a complete courtier, with all that implies.

Because of his high regard for Becket, Henry made arrangements to elevate him to the office of High Chancellor and Preceptor to his son Prince Henry. Presumably to prepare him to carry out his new duties as Chancellor, Theobald, the Archbishop of Canterbury, arranged for him to go to Bologna in Italy to study law at the university there. No doubt his studies would have been wide-ranging, encompassing aspects of canon as well as civil law. This would have widened Becket's mental and moral horizons beyond anything he might have previously experienced. Within a few years of his return from Italy his mentor, Theobald, died, leaving the post as head of the English church vacant.

Henry was frustrated by the continual intrusion of ecclesiastical law. In effect he wanted all miscreants tried and sentenced according to secular justice. At that time, any persons connected to the Church, in even the most menial way, came under the protection of the Church authorities whose decisions overrode those of the civil authorities. With the power to remove a miscreant from the jurisdiction of the king's court they could and sometimes did grant absolution, even for crimes of the most heinous type such as murder or rape. In passing judgement they exercised absolute discretion in deciding whether to accept or disregard evidence submitted, even by eye-witnesses. This was a source of deep discontent among the peasantry. Henry himself felt strongly that it was diminishing his authority and was anxious to end the practice.

It must have seemed to Henry that he had suddenly been presented with a solution to his conflict with the Church. If he installed Becket as the new Archbishop of Canterbury he would have an ally in the hierarchy of the Church who would be willing and able to argue his case with the Pope. In 1162 he appointed Becket to the Archbishopric of Canterbury and in doing so he set in chain a sequence of events which he could never have imagined would have such far-reaching repercussions. For one thing, he had raised Becket to a station superior to the king himself in some respects.

In addition, a transformation had taken place in the personality of Becket. Always an extremist in his behaviour, he went from living a life of extravagant opulence to one of extraordinary austerity, and became a zealous champion of the Church, opposed to the aggressions and encroachments of the king whose policy of subordinating the Church to civil power was paramount. One of his first acts was to demand from the king the return to the Church of Rochester and its castle, as entrusted by Henry I to Archbishop Corbeuil in 1125. He included in his demand many other estates which had been sequestrated during the period of the disciplining of the barons. Following this he rejected Henry's assumption that henceforth ecclesiastical law would be subordinated to civil law. Henry reacted furiously to what he saw as betrayal, and proceeded to draw up his own proclamations.

Tensions began to build to a climax when a code of laws was presented by Henry on January 1164 to a council of barons and prelates. The meeting took place at a village

51

named Clarendon in Wiltshire and became known as The Constitutions of Clarendon. The laws were eventually distilled into 16 articles, which were ostensibly a re-statement of 'the ancient customs of the realm', but the nub of the document was to actually enshrine in law the supremacy of the State over that of the Church. All ecclesiastical appointments were to come under the control of the State. Any appeal to Rome was to be subject to approval by the king and ecclesiastical personnel would be unable to leave the country without royal permission.

It was argued that as Becket was supreme head of the Church in England, and directly under the ecumenical supervision of Rome, the conditions being proposed by the king were unacceptable. Henry was implacable on the subject and forced him to sign, albeit under duress. Becket did manage to convey a report of the matter to Pope Alexander III, outlining his anxieties, with the result that the Pope refused to accept the constitutions, whereupon Becket was vindicated in retracting his signature to the document. The ensuing meetings between the king and Becket ended in serious dispute. Evidence of the profound nature of the conflict was evinced when the archbishop felt obliged to flee to France from where he petitioned, and received, the Pope's protection and support. After much negotiation, a form of reconciliation between the two parties was believed to have been achieved, whereupon Becket returned to England.

Becket continued thereafter to defy royal authority on matters where the Church claimed precedence and believed himself to be insulated against further royal oppression. Matters took a more ominous twist when in a rash outburst Henry railed against the continual trouble caused to him by Becket. This happened in the presence of witnesses and four of them, the barons Reginald Fitz-Urse, William de Tracey, Hugh de Morville and Richard de Breto, were induced to go immediately to Canterbury and confront Becket within the cathedral itself. We will never know if they thought he could be subdued by threats alone or whether his defiance incited them beyond forbearance, but they were unable to quell his spiritual beliefs by argument. These warriors, whose brains and instincts resided in their scabbards, unsheathed their swords and struck him down, leaving his brains scattered on the floor. To imagine they were representing the wishes of the king by this violation was astonishing. Although he possessed all the wilfulness of a mediaeval king, Henry was fully aware of the limits to which even he might go. He had devoted his reign to establishing law and order. Until that time, by following this route, his reign had been a fruitful one, bringing prosperity and order to the country.

The reaction was immediate. Becket was instantly acclaimed as a martyr, while Henry denied vigorously that he had sanctioned the murder – he had merely complained vehemently against the continual opposition he encountered from Becket. That it was overheard and misconstrued by the perpetrators was not his fault. In various ways Henry was humiliated by the Pope and spent many years trying penitently to make amends. He was forced to withdraw the main clauses in The Constitutions of Clarendon in favour of the Church. Becket was canonised in 1172 by Pope Alexander III. His shrine became a favourite place of pilgrimage for centuries after.

Henry died on 6 July 1189. His most lasting achievement was the introduction of common law and the partitioning of England into four judiciary districts, with regular visits by circuit judges to dispense the king's laws, a system that was much acclaimed. The jury system effectively bypassed the local barons who had previously exercised their own tyrannical rule. It seems that the origins of trial by jury are not attributable to any particular period or person, but to his credit Henry appears to have considered juries important, and included them in his system of justice and government. All in all he was judged to have been a successful sovereign.

Richard the Lionheart

Richard was the third son of Henry II by Eleanor of Aquitaine. He was born at Beaumont Palace in Oxfordshire in 1157 and crowned king in 1189 after the death of his father.

A man of great faults and sometimes great virtues, he was not altogether deserving of the almost unreserved acclaim attached to his reign, due in large part in recent times to Hollywood film-makers. In their medium he is portrayed as the essential saviour of England and the fount of all justice and honesty. In fact, although he was born at Oxford he spent almost his whole life outside the country. He was no English patriot, spending most of his time in France and less than a year in England after his coronation. The bulk of that period he spent trying to raise money to fund a crusade to the Holy Land. A series of punitive taxes on the general population was levied and as a supplement he released William the Lion from prison and restored him to the throne of Scotland for 10,000 marks.

His alliance with the French King Philip against his own father was a particularly degenerate act for a man whose code was professed to be that of chivalry. He committed this deed to further his overriding ambition to lead a crusade to Jerusalem. To finance it, he once said that he would willingly sell the City of London. General opinion is that he was not even as effective a ruler as his brother John, who was hardly renowned for his ability. His fame rested on his undoubted bravery in war. His refusal to cooperate with others resulted in the break-up of the forces attempting to hold Jerusalem. First he quarrelled with his erstwhile ally and friend, Philip Augustus of France, partly because he had reneged on a previous commitment to marry Philip's sister Alice, and instead had married Berengaria of Navarre. The other problem which caused the rift within the combined crusading forces arose from Richard's dismissive attitude towards the leadership qualities of both Philip and Leopold of Austria. His attitude was so offensive they both decided to quit the scene and return home, thus bringing about the collapse of the Third Crusade.

Richard paid dearly for the insult he offered to Leopold of Austria. Returning from Jerusalem, the ship on which he was travelling sank and he was forced to make the remainder of the journey overland. While passing through Germany, Leopold was informed and took him prisoner. A ransom of 150,000 marks was demanded for his release. It amounted to practically three times the revenue of the whole of England, and the resulting taxation was severe and caused great hardship and suffering. The churches were also denuded of their holy relics and ornaments. Notwithstanding the suffering he had caused to the populace, Richard soon left England for France to engage in more vainglorious minor wars with seemingly little purpose.

Richard died in 1199 in France at the age of 42, of a wound received during a siege of Chalus, and was buried at Fontevrault.

John

Richard's brother John was born in 1167 and ascended the throne in 1199, to begin a reign of 17 years. John has been cast in history as the archetypal 'baddie', mainly as a result of the harsh and uncaring treatment of his subjects during his reign. He was nicknamed 'Lackland' because his father did not initially endow him with any territory, which was strange because he was always reputed to be the favourite son. The expense of the Third Crusade and the ransom exacted by Leopold had drained England's coffers dry. In spite of the hardship being experienced throughout the country John continued to impose more punitive taxes, dispossessing those who could not pay. No doubt he required money to pay for the defence of his French possessions but his greedy and avaricious nature meant that he carried the practice too far, causing greater suffering to the peasantry.

It was all to no avail as by 1204 the French King Philip Augustus had bit by bit deprived John of Normandy, Maine and Anjou. To accentuate John's problems the barons in these domains were beginning to transfer their allegiances away from him and were content to be closer to the burgeoning French court.

Apparently having learned nothing from the experience of his father's humiliation at the hands of the Church authorities, when in 1207 Stephen Langton was nominated by Pope Innocent III to the office of Archbishop of Canterbury, John refused to accept him. The outcome was roughly as before. Differences between John and Rome grew greater until the king ordered seizure of many Church lands. By 1209 the Church and all of its services had ceased to function and John was excommunicated. Finally he was threatened with deposition by the Pope. In effect England could have become the subject of a crusade under the blessing of the Pope. John finally yielded and like his father before him suffered the fate of abject surrender accompanied by painful and humiliating penances. All his obstinacy had been to no avail because in 1213 he had to accede to Stephen Langton being appointed Archbishop of Canterbury.

In an attempt to regain his lost provinces in France John allied himself with Flanders and the German Emperor Otto IV. Their joint forces clashed with the French on the 27 July 1214 at Bouvines, near Lille, and were heavily defeated.

The combination of despotic government and extortionate taxation had been a source of discontent within the baronial class for a long time. Their exasperation was such that while John was away in France they formulated a plan to oust him. We know that this class of warrior was more renowned for battle than for deep thought, but even they acknowledged that what they had in mind had dangerous ramifications and would need to be sanctioned by the Church. Knowing also that John had already alienated himself from Archbishop Langton they took the risk of taking him into their collective confidence and asked for his aid and advice.

Their instincts were on this occasion to be applauded. Langton probably counselled them against action that was too drastic and which would plunge the country into chaos, as well as playing into the hands of those domestic enemies who would take advantage of such a situation. In his counselling he no doubt impressed upon them that as King John had just received a severe defeat at the hands of the French he would not be able to match the forces arraigned against him. It was therefore imperative that any concessions extorted from him were seen to be principled and just. The objective was not to bring down the king but to persuade him to act and observe laws which applied to all without exception. By so doing it could not be claimed later that illegal conditions were extracted under duress nor by treasonable act.

A document known as the *Magna Carta Libertatum* (Great Charter of Liberties) listing their demands was presented, by a confederation of barons to the king at Runnymede on 15 June 1215, and he signed it without delay. The nobles themselves were probably unaware of the wider implications of the *Charter* in that it represented a general declaration of entitlement to justice from a king regardless of rank or class. Not even the influence of Pope Innocent III, who declared the *Magna Carta* invalid and excommunicated the barons who supported it, could expunge its import and repercussions. This document has been the founding philosophy of every democratic society since that time.

King John had no intention of keeping his word, and afterwards successfully appealed to the Pope against the validity of the *Charter*. This was surprising in view of the fact that the document contained a clause to maintain the right of the Church to make all ecclesiastical appointments, which John had fought so hard to nullify. Now with the Pope on his side, to abrogate the *Charter*, John chose his usual approach and raised an army to take revenge against those who had enforced it. So severe were his attacks on them that the barons invited the heir to the French crown, later to become Louis VIII of France, to accept the crown of England. He landed at Sandwich on 30 May 1216 at the head of a large army and was received as lawful sovereign. This unexpected tactic presented King John with another and more powerful opponent. Naturally, he resisted their intrusion and a number of sporadic encounters ensued. Possibly he was overwhelmed by the added exertions and pressures he faced, but everything was brought to a halt on 18 October 1216 with the sudden death of John at the age of 49.

Now that John was out of the way the nobles were facing a new dilemma. They no longer needed the assistance of the French, nor did they wish to be part of France. Louis had come on the firm understanding that the throne was his for the taking. When the barons reversed their invitation it was received with outrage and resulted in conflict which lasted for some time. Nevertheless, the invading army became isolated among its erstwhile allies, putting it at serious disadvantage. Eventually talks took place culminating in a compensatory payment to Louis and he and his mercenaries left.

Robin Hood/The longbow

Robin Hood is portrayed as having been vigorously active against the brutality of John's reign, which is a probability. His band of outlaws is also supposed to have contained a Friar Tuck, a grey friar. This would

---

have been impossible because the Franciscan order was not founded until 1210 and did not reach England until 1220, whereas John died in 1216. It was, however, the probable period when the English longbow, made from yew and with its legendary power and accuracy, was in regular use.

Henry III

Born in 1207, Henry was only 9 years of age when he ascended the throne in 1216 and was overseen by advisers and wards until he came of age. During this period the question of the invaders under the French Prince Louis had to be resolved and their remaining adherents finally shepherded from the country.

Henry was pious and learned but his nature embraced most of the least desirable characteristics one might wish to find in a ruler. This latest in the line was just as weak, untrustworthy and ineffectual as the two who had preceded him. He was also a slow learner, and replicated many of the mistakes made by his predecessors. Admittedly he inherited a fairly run-down treasury, but he then followed the well-worn path of extortionate taxation, failing to embark on promised reforms and compounding his unpopularity by his oppressive abuses of forest law on which the rural peasantry largely depended to graze their animals or occasionally hunt small or large game.

He married Eleanor of Provence who persuaded him to fill his court with her relatives and elevate them to the highest positions. In spite of the fact that Parliament continued to fund his extravagant lifestyle, on the condition of ratifying the Great Charter, he repeatedly reneged from his promises.

A generally dismissive attitude toward the ruling classes

fomented a growing dissatisfaction, not least by requiring them to present their pleas to foreign cronies who now occupied the highest offices within the State. Oddly enough it was the king's brother-in-law Simon de Montfort, himself a foreigner, who emerged as the leader of the discontented nobles. After a number of meetings which proved to be ineffectual the parties became determined to bring about a conclusion by force. On 14 May 1264 a battle was fought at Lewes, Sussex, when the king was defeated, and he and his son Edward were taken prisoner.

Henry retained his position as monarch but he was forced to attend a 'Parlement' or Parliament which contained two knights from each shire and two burgesses from selected towns. This was due to the persistence of Simon de Montfort. He is sometimes claimed to be the founder of the House of Commons but other sources reject this by pointing out that regular representation of cities and boroughs in Parliament did not start until 1295. It was however a vision of de Montfort to make this practice part of the normal system of government.

Problems developed between leaders in the de Montford faction arising from the fact that the violent and autocratic de Montfort was deemed to be overbearing and impossible to deal with on an equal basis. On the other hand, it could have been that the barons realised that he was taking them down a road inclined towards Parliamentary government, which in itself was a threat to their feudal overlordship. Taking advantage of their lack of cohesion Henry once again managed to muster support against the nobles and a battle was fought at Evesham in 1265. Simon de Montfort was killed and the king regained his throne.

As a king, Henry III was in most things a failure, and it is a shame that he reigned for so long – 56 years in all. To his credit, probably because he was a pious man, he was dedicated to the building or improvement of churches. He commissioned the architects and master masons who rebuilt Westminster Abbey to build a new cathedral at Salisbury and remodel many other English cathedrals in a more refined or elaborate style.

Salisbury Cathedral

Salisbury Cathedral unfortunately appears to have been built on ground susceptible to moisture and never an ideal site for such a monumental building. Around the end of the twentieth century, examination showed that movement in the foundations had taken place and needed urgent attention to prevent further slippage that could destabilise the entire building. The techniques used to counteract this possibility were similar to those used to address the problem with the leaning tower of Pisa some years earlier: underpinning the foundations by gradual injection of stabilising material. The modern city of Salisbury (New Sarum) is situated on a plain about two miles from the original town, castle and cathedral, from where it was removed in 1219. The foundation stone of the new cathedral was laid in 1220.

A significant omission by Henry after he regained power was that conditions regarding the convening of Parliament forced upon him by de Montfort during the rebellion were not rescinded. They embodied profound portents for the future, which when melded with ideas already in the public perception such as the *Magna Carta* were powerful vehicles which would one day lead to constitutional monarchy. Only today with the benefit of hindsight are we able to appreciate this. As a king of the period Henry could not imagine that by tactically 'allowing' Parliament to continue, agreement to the procedure of the changed system of governing the country was implicit.

Roger Bacon

Roger Bacon, one of the most original thinkers of that age, was born in 1214. He was a significant figure of the time having studied at the universities of Oxford and Paris and received the degree of Doctor of Theology. He excelled as an experimental chemist and was in many respects way ahead of his time from a scientific point of view. He wrote the *Opus Major* which dealt with experimental science, metaphysics and optics. In the latter he made significant strides. He is credited by some as being the first to discover gunpowder. Others maintain that China was the source but the working life of Bacon was coming to a close about the time that Marco Polo and his father first visited China in 1274 and he was dead the year before they returned to Europe in 1295, which rules out any opportunity they would have had to impart any information on the subject.

Because of the jealousy and hatred Bacon's work instilled in his fellow monks, the Church had him incarcerated in a Paris monastery without paper or writing instruments for more than 15 years. In spite of this he demonstrated his knowledge of geography and astronomy by explaining the errors of the calendar. His suggestions for correcting them were reputed to be very close to the truth.

Edward I (Long shanks)

Born on 7 July 1239 at Winchester, when Edward's father died in 1272 he automatically inherited the crown. A man of action and decisiveness and a soldier of distinction, he was someone with a respect for the law and its application within good government. It was clear by his action in creating his Model Parliament in 1295 that he saw considerable merit and advantage in governing by consent. He brought together the nobility, knights merchants, burgesses, clergy and land-owners in the manner proposed by de Montfort. However, no ruler of the time acted entirely, if at all, altruistically and he was no exception. He needed money to introduce reforms in administration or enhance those already introduced by Henry II. Circuit judges, courts of the king's bench, the Court of Equity and the Chancery Court were all set up to enable litigants to engage in specialised areas never before available to them.

By co-opting the land-owning classes into the regular practice of government Edward was making them aware also of the cost involved, which in turn lubricated the machinery of exacting taxes to which, having learned their necessity, they could hardly disagree. They realised that if they wanted a fairer and safer society with better conditions then they must share the financial burden.

Until the advent of Llewelyn ap Gruffud, although there were a number of lesser leaders of smaller kingdoms within the isolated fastnesses of mountainous Wales, none had managed to unite them as he seemed to do. Instead of relying on isolated raids on Norman outposts or settlements he decided to confront them as an independent ruler. He made his first defiant gesture when, in 1272 Edward demanded homage to be rendered from the domain of Llewelyn, he refused. It should be borne in mind that south Wales, at this juncture, had been so heavily populated by Normans, English and Flemish settlers, all protected by Norman castles, that the domain of Llewelyn was confined to the areas of Snowdonia and Anglesey. In an act of retaliation and defiance of Henry III Llewelyn captured Shrewsbury and also made some successful inroads into South Wales. Edward invaded in 1272, forcing Llewelyn to accept terms of surrender. Five years later Llewelyn led another revolt but was killed near Builth. Edward then annexed Wales to England and its independence ended. Vigorous castle building in Wales ensued to secure the peace.

Edward was invited to adjudicate in the selection of a king in Scotland, he chose John Balliol. The high-handed manner in which he conducted the ceremony angered the Anglo/Norman rulers of Scotland as well as the ordinary people, causing them to start a Scottish rebellion. John Balliol was crowned at Scone in 1292 but he and his associates felt he had been humiliated by conceding too many powers to the English king. After a period he declared Scotland independent and formed a military alliance with France, which inspired two incursions by Edward's forces, the second of which culminated in a rout of the Scottish army at Spottismuir. Balliol subsequently abdicated.

At this point, from an unexpected source came disaffection with the situation. William Wallace came to the fore as someone taking on the challenge laid down by Balliol and his declaration of independence. He became a partisan leader, eventually acquiring a large army which in 1297 was besieging the castle of Dundee when he received information that an army under the Earl of Surrey was marching to Stirling. He immediately diverted his forces to meet them and at the battle of Stirling Bridge defeated them. Lord Cressingham, who was accompanying Surrey is said to have been flayed alive by Wallace who had a belt made from his skin – such was the mediaeval mind.

Wallace then invaded northern England a number of times,

devastating the countryside and taking many women prisoners north as slaves, indicating that justice was not his sole objective.

The following year Edward personally led the attack on Wallace who retreated before him using what we would nowadays call a scorched earth policy, destroying everything which might possibly be of use to the enemy, even the cattle and cottages of his own people. Eventually Edward caught up with Wallace's army at Falkirk and routed them, but Wallace escaped. Although he was hunted not much was heard of him afterwards until he was finally apprehended by Sir John Monteith, governor of Dunbarton Castle, and taken to London where he was executed.

The Lake of Monteith

The Lake of Monteith is said to be the only lake in Scotland – all the others are known as lochs. The distinction is said to mark Sir John Monteith's alleged treachery to the Scottish cause. This is quite plausible but the fact is that the nobility of the time in Scotland had the best of both worlds. They were owners of large estates in England dating back to 1066 which they gradually added to in Scotland. It was in their interests to retain the status quo.

Once Wallace had inflamed the situation and enlisted the passion of the ordinary people, independence was the only course those people would follow. After his death the powerful Norman aristocratic oligarchy existing there realised that the next Scottish king would again come from one of their number and de Brus (Bruce) was their choice.

At this point Edward I assembled another army and marched

north but he was taken ill on the way and upon reaching a place named Burgh-on-Sands near Carlisle in 1307 he died. At this critical time it must have been heartening news to the Scots that this formidable warrior leader was no longer a threat and had been replaced by a callow and narcissistic youth. Unfortunately for England it was now left in the custodianship of this effete boy of little, if any, competence, military or otherwise.

Edward's legacy was to form, in 1295 at Westminster, what became known as the 'Model Parliament'. Because of this he has been acclaimed by some as the father of the 'Mother of all Parliaments'. His unfulfilled ambition was to unite all corners of Britain under one national identity, legislative body and crown, similar to that finally achieved in France. In addition, during his reign Oxford University College was established, with Balliol College following in 1268 and Merton College in 1274.

Edward II

Born in 1284 at Carnarvon Castle and taking the throne in 1307, Edward II was possibly one of the most effete and ineffectual of rulers ever to succeed to the throne of England. He surrounded himself with favourites of the worst type, in particular a dissolute and effeminate French nobleman, Piers Gaveston. His hedonism and general indolence knew no bounds. Without any vestige of discipline, he was totally useless as a soldier which, at that time, was an essential part of the duties of a king. The sudden death of his father catapulted him into the position of being leader of a large army prepared to put down the challenge of Bruce who had gained the throne in Scotland. This vacillating and militarily inexperienced young wastrel continued into Scotland in 1307 at the head of the army which his father had assembled.

Upon reaching Cumnock in Ayrshire, a march of little more than a day from Carlisle, he for no apparent reason decided to return home without accomplishing anything. He dismissed his troops and returned to a life of self-indulgence.

Meantime, in his quest for the Scottish throne, Bruce had either eliminated his rivals or as his influence grew they had joined his cause. An infamous occasion during this period was in 1306 when he invited John Comyn of Badenoch, who was the head of probably the most powerful Anglo-Norman family in Scotland, to discuss matters surrounding the campaign against England and their respective claims to the Scottish crown. They agreed to meet in the Greyfriars church at Dumfries, a place regarded as a haven of neutrality and a natural safeguard against any violation of trust. It proved not to be for Comyn, for during their exchanges Bruce killed him, thus removing the main competitor for the crown vacated by Balliol. Under the religious ethics of the period Bruce would normally have been excommunicated for the desecration of a church but the incident passed without demur. Also surprising is that Bishop Wishart, without seeking advice or permission from the Pope, gave Bruce immediate absolution for the crime. A possible reason may have been that during this period the papacy was in some turmoil and the Pope of the time had antagonised France. The French King Philip the Fair in his exasperation over the matter had kidnapped the Pope (Boniface VIII) and forcibly transferred him to Avignon. The See remained vacant from 1305 for just over two years.

During the seven years following the death of Edward I Bruce was active. He strengthened his army considerably and won back almost all the occupied territories. In direct contrast Edward II was engaged in his usual dissipating lifestyle, totally ignoring his duties as a monarch. He showered even more gifts on his favourite; so much that the barons were so incensed that they rebelled, took Gaveston prisoner and executed him.

Bruce was about to gain control of Stirling castle so Edward decided to make another foray into Scotland to relieve the defenders. This he undertook in spite of his lack of ability, experience or real military skill, against a well prepared and battle-hardened campaigner fighting on his home ground. The outcome was a comprehensive defeat of Edward's army in 1314 at a place called Bannockburn, and this shored up the call for Scottish independence. On the evidence of this victory and its portents it was considered a perfect opportunity for Bruce and his advisers to submit a petition to the Pope for recognition of independence.

Undeterred by the fate of Piers Gaveston, Edward then transferred his affections to Hugh Despenser, another equally dissolute and imprudent young man who recklessly replicated the behaviour which had cost his predecessor his life. This time it was exacerbated by the actions of his father, also named Hugh Despenser. Hugh senior, although he had been a loyal supporter of the royal house, was not of high ranking nobility but, as a result of the relationship between his son and the king, he began to exert undue influence at court which alienated him even further from the higher baronial class. He was now encroaching on ground which the barons jealously guarded as their prerogative.

Edward's wife, Isabella, disgusted by what had occurred within her marriage contrived a plan by which she and her son were able to make a journey to visit her brother Charles IV, King of France. It was unlikely that she had any intention of returning to England to try to resuscitate her failed marriage. Nevertheless she was still the rightful queen and the offence she had received was unforgivable. Convinced that her husband was not governing as he should, and seething over her treatment, she decided to strike back. While in France she formed a liaison with an exiled baron, Roger Mortimer, Earl of March, becoming his mistress. Together they collected an army partly composed of disaffected exiles and equally unhappy barons in England, and supplemented by a force of mercenaries provided by the Count of Hainault. This army then landed in Suffolk. In the space of a few months they had overwhelmed the supporters of the king. The Despensers, both father and son, were executed. The king was incarcerated first in Kenilworth and finally in Berkeley Castle where he was murdered on 21 September 1327.

Edward III

Edward III was nominated by Edward II as his successor. Born in 1312, he took the throne in 1327 and reigned for 50 years. As he was only 15 when he was crowned, his early years as king were overseen by a council of regency. However, true power lay with Mortimer, his mother's lover, who dominated the council and therefore the country. Mortimer was an unscrupulous and oppressive man whose misuse of his powers led to a general confederacy of powerful nobles against him. With the assent of the young king, Mortimer was arrested on 10 October 1330 and executed. Edward's mother Isabella was deprived of her influence but, although she was equally culpable in deposing and disposing of her husband in conspiracy with her lover, Edward, it is said, treated her courteously and considerately. She went into retirement and later entered a convent in France.

Edward was a man of enormous energy and an enthusiastic soldier, much like his grandfather. As a minor he had been coerced by his mother and Mortimer into signing the Treaty of Northampton in 1328, agreeing to the independence of Scotland, an action which still rankled with him years later, especially so as the Scots never seemed to be placated and in league with their allies the French were again attacking and laying waste to northern England.

Edward decided to confront the situation in the north where

the Scots army had occupied Berwick-on-Tweed. He laid siege to the town, the governor of which had agreed to surrender if not relieved by 20 July 1333. On 19 July a large Scottish army led by the regent of Scotland, Archibald Douglas, attacked the English army at Halidon Hill a few miles north of Berwick, but the Scots were totally routed, losing about 10,000 men. The regent and a number of his earls were among the dead.

Eager to recapture lands in France which had been lost during the reign of his father, Edward now turned his attention there. He received the support of the Flanders weavers who desperately needed English wool to feed their industry. The workers in this region had developed great skill in the production of high quality carpets, tapestries, clothing and associated products, therefore a steady supply of high grade wool was essential.

The French had banned trade with England, in particular the importation of wool, vital to the English economy, and were blockading the ports. To do this they had assembled an enormous fleet of ships from allies and mercenaries to prevent a landing of any type, commercial or military.

From an English point of view it was imperative to overcome the blockade to glean the revenue from the wool trade without which it was impossible to finance military operations against France and their allies the Scots, who were usually enlisted and financed by the French king to attack England whenever English armies were engaged in hostilities in France. It was therefore essential to gain access to Bruges and the surrounding territories, but first they had to penetrate the enormous armada of ships barring the way.

Fortunately for Edward in 1338/9, prior to the Battle of Sluys, the artisans of the region of Bruges, Ghent and the surrounding area had risen in revolt against the suffocating control over their lives being exercised by the French. The severe restrictions on imports of wool from England was seriously undermining their living standards but, as frequently happens, along comes a leader whose convictions were strong enough to challenge unjust authority. Such a man was James van Artevelde, a rich merchant of Ghent who had little to gain from taking sides with the working peasantry, but nevertheless did just that. He mobilised the common folk to rebel and with the primitive weaponry available to them they overcame the French garrisons in the area. Van Artevelde knew that it was one thing to gain a minor victory but totally different to maintain the position against an adversary who would mount the inevitable reprisals. They appealed to Edward to invade and establish himself as monarch of several of the states. He was after all married to Phillippa, the daughter of the Count of Hainault, who controlled one of the areas adversely affected by the ban.

The English, at that time, were not reckoned to have more than a second-rate naval force, far inferior to their opponents. The French and their allies, with superior fleets, were constantly harrying, burning and pillaging the towns on the south coast of England, in addition to sinking and capturing English ships in the Channel. Disregarding the risks and the condemnation of his intentions by senior figures in England, Edward decided that the only way was to attack head on, even though his puny force was given little chance of victory. He did, however, have that weapon which had been developed over the previous century and was becoming a decisive factor in many encounters, the English longbow. This weapon had been perfected into one of deadly accuracy and he employed it as the mainstay of his attack on the French fleet by packing his ships with expert marksmen.

The Battle of Sluys in June 1340 near Landenberg overturned all the odds when the little ships of Edward's force sailed straight into and among the defending fleet. Before the defenders could launch an attack of their own a hail of arrows of pinpoint accuracy had cleared their decks of troops allowing the ships to be taken by boarding parties. The battle ended in overwhelming victory for the English who destroyed or took over 200 ships belonging to the French, Spanish and Genoese and opened the way into Flanders and inevitably France. It ended the dominance of the Channel for ever by the French and Spanish seamen and was one of the first decisive victories for England in the Hundred Years War, 1338–1453.

In 1333 the devastating power of the longbow was demonstrated once more when a Scots army was assembled to invade England. They reached Berwick-on-Tweed and were confronted by an English force which included a large company of bowmen. The ensuing battle saw the Scottish army routed with losses reckoned to be in excess of four thousand men and including many of their nobility.

In 1346, Edward III, accompanied by his 16-year-old son Edward (the 'Black Prince', born 15 June 1330, died 1376), crossed to France and on 26 August was confronted by a large and heavily equipped French army at a place called Crécy, about eight or nine miles north of Abbeville. The outcome of the Battle of Crécy shocked the European nations with the scale of the defeat inflicted on the French. Of the opposing forces there were said to be at least 30,000 infantry and 1,200 horse left dead on the field. Among them were the King of Bohemia, the Count of Alencon, the Count of Flanders and many of the French nobility. According to other records, late reinforcements, marching to bolster the French ranks, were intercepted on the roads in the vicinity and destroyed, the total almost equalling that of the main host. Altogether a disastrous day for the French. The young Black Prince commanded part of the army that day with great distinction. It was reported that the English had destroyed the might of France with the loss of fewer than 50 of their own soldiers.

Edward then led his army to Calais and laid siege to the

castle. This lasted for about a year until in 1347 they capitulated, ultimately worn down by starvation. Queen Phillippa, the wife of Edward, made an impassioned plea for the lives of the Burghers of Calais to be spared. Under the terms of war at the time the lives of the leaders of a castle or garrison were spared only if they capitulated without offering undue defence, but on this occasion the queen pleaded extenuating circumstances and successfully intervened on their behalf.

In 1346, while some of these events were taking place, the Scots under the leadership of David Bruce II, believing that the French campaign had denuded England of its fighting men and in support of their French allies, invaded England, indiscriminately killing and devastating the countryside. An English army set out to confront them and they met at a place near the city of Durham named Neville's Cross. The Scottish army was heavily defeated and King David taken prisoner. He remained so for 11 years under ransom and was not released until 1357 under the terms of the Treaty of Berwick.

In 1356 Edward the Black Prince, now a seasoned warrior, won several battles to recapture territory. The most telling of these was the famous victory over the French at Poitiers, when the French enjoyed a supremacy of numbers of about five to one. Because they were facing such overwhelming odds the Black Prince had offered to withdraw and make reparations, but as the French considered themselves secure with their massive advantage in numbers the offer was rejected; therefore the English were forced to fight a desperate rearguard action. One of the generals assisting the French that day was William Douglas, a veteran of the Scottish-English wars. In this battle, against all expectations, the French were utterly routed and King John was captured. This meant that the English now had the kings of both Scotland and France in their custody which undoubtedly added to

Edward's bargaining power. He had initially claimed the throne of France but this was merely an opening gambit designed to provoke a reaction and he was content to rescind it in favour of his real intent, which was to regain his former lands. In 1360 the Treaty of Bretigny was formulated on these terms and lands amounting to a quarter of all France was conceded to England and ransoms of incredible amounts paid – some, like that of the French king, were so large they had to be rendered in instalments and the alliance with Scotland had to be renounced.

Despite his successes, Edward's campaigns had virtually drained England's coffers. The costs of prosecuting the war, including subsidies given to the people of Flanders, had depended on heavy taxation on all classes of English society, particularly the merchants. Apparently this did not go unnoticed by the king because it was in the aftermath that Parliament was divided to add a House of Commons. He had certainly recognised the importance of cooperation with the nobility in the peaceful governance of the country, but without diminishing their role he and his advisers obviously needed to acknowledge the growing influence of commerce and the powerful figures it was beginning to uncover. It had also become apparent that during this era the king and his counsellors were finding themselves more in accord with the English than the French. This was demonstrated in 1362 when the parliamentary proceedings began to be conducted in the English language.

In France, Edward and his son had recovered the lands to which they originally laid claim and more besides, but their exploits were to come to nought in the light of subsequent events. The Black Prince won fame and renown by his exceptional military prowess but he died in 1376, a year before his father, leaving his son Richard to inherit a crown bereft of most of the lands in France in competition for which so many had died.

The changing shape of the French monarchy in relation to the vastly differing regions was the main reason contributing to the recapture of territory previously held by the Anglo-Normans. In earlier times rulers such as Burgundy, Piedmont, Savoy and Aquitaine operated almost as equals to the king, throwing in with whomever offered them most advantage, the king being simply the titular head of State. Successive French monarchs convinced them that while they apparently enjoyed a semblance of independence it left them somewhat isolated if they themselves were under attack. This statesman-like approach cleverly brought about the gradual conversion of the regional oligarchies, capable of opposing or switching allegiance away from the French king, to an aristocracy with closer liaison to the monarchy providing mutual defence. Another cogent and persuasive argument was that some territory had been gained by English nobility through astute marriages into French families thus diluting the opportunities for their own extended progeny to retain possession. The question of inheritance is always a subject capable of arousing passionate resentment. It also offers powerful motivation to unite differing factions in common cause.

Collectively, all these considerations probably played a part in guiding the French nobles on a path toward nationhood. After all, France, with a population of at least four times that of England, by acting in concert, could absorb the remaining independent regions and hold them against further incursions. So it proved. Neither would they be ignorant of the cost to the Anglo-Normans of repeatedly taking armies to France.

Pressure on the treasury resurrected a dispute between Edward III and the papacy over the question of the vassalage and tribute which had been exacted from King John. Edward rejected them both and was supported by the English Parliament. John Wycliffe, a noted scholar, had written several papers on the subject, in support of the sovereign and against the Church. His patriotic stance came to the notice of John of Gaunt, Duke of Lancaster, who then became his patron. In 1374 he was one of the commissioners sent to Bruges to discuss the delicate subjects of praemunire and the statutes with a representative of the Pope.

John Wycliffe

An English reformer, born about 1320 at Richmond, Yorkshire, and educated at Oxford, Wycliffe became master of Balliol College and also a doctor of theology and teacher of divinity in the university. He was a thorn in the side of agents of the Church during the reign of Edward III and continued to be so under Richard II.

He accused the Pope of various improprieties including covetousness, simony and tyranny, and generally attacked him. The Pope then petitioned the king to arraign Wycliffe. Wycliffe was cautioned and placed under an injunction to discontinue his anti-papal utterances. In the time-honoured way, opinions issued by a respected and powerful public figure always carry weight and the claims and statements denouncing the malpractices of the Church and particularly the Pope began to circulate. Wycliffe's insistence that Englishmen should by right be entitled to read the Bible in their own language struck a chord with the common people.

In 1377 Wycliffe was summoned to appear in front of a convocation at St Paul's Cathedral to account for his behaviour. He was attended by some of his powerful friends, the Duke of Lancaster, John of Gaunt, among them. Apparently the bishop and the duke took great exception to certain remarks made by the other and punches were thrown, the whole meeting breaking up in some confusion.

Later that same year the Pope renewed the attack on Wycliffe by issuing three Bulls, one each to the primate, the king and the University of Oxford insisting that action be taken to curb him. These proceedings were drawn to a conclusion when the queen mother decided that Wycliffe should be censured with an injunction to cease preaching the obnoxious doctrines.

It did not cause much inconvenience to Wycliffe at the time because he was heavily engaged in translating the Bible from the vulgate (a very ancient version of the Latin scriptures) into English. He was helped in this endeavour by some of his friends. Further disapproval from the Church was incurred. In the past they had enjoyed sole access to the biblical text and guarded the privilege jealously. However, members of the public received it favourably and saw it was as an incentive to learn to read their everyday language which was gradually changing.

Wycliffe's literary output was prodigious, in both Latin and English, influencing opinion on the Continent as well as in England. He was instrumental in defining Protestant thought and belief. A free thinker and plain speaker he, without doubt, raised the platform which afterwards supported the Reformation. In doing all this he certainly laid claim to being the father of English prose.

William Langland

William Langland was born about 1332 at Cleobury-Mortimer, Shropshire. He was an early English poet who composed the poem *The Vision of William* concerning Piers Plowman, about 1362. This work deals with the worldliness and corruption in the Church at that time, and gives valuable insights into English life of the period as well as providing material for the study of English in its early forms. In particular it highlights how the Church played a significant part in restricting the freedoms of the lower classes.

Geoffrey Chaucer

Chaucer's estimated year of birth is 1340 in London. He was the recipient of a very sound education at one of the good London schools of the time, rather than at one of the two ancient universities. He was well connected at court and served as a page to the Duke of Clarence and his wife, the Countess of Ulster, during visits to Flanders and Cologne in 1338. He was a soldier in the army of Edward III and in 1359 was taken prisoner in France, his ransom being paid by the king. Afterwards he spent about 10 years as a diplomat but his claim to fame lies in his poetry. Undoubtedly his varied experiences allied to a brilliant mind filled with an unusual mix of humour, sensitivity and rustic earthiness led to the development of his genius. He was the first (and some say the best) to be buried in Poet's Corner in Westminster Abbey, in 1400.

Richard II

Born at Bordeaux in 1367 and succeeding to the throne in 1377, Richard II suffered the usual fate of those taking the crown as a minor. He knew he was king but always under the thumb of those risibly described as advisers when in actual fact they ran the affairs of state to suit themselves, John of Gaunt in particular.

Richard was a weak, temperamental boy given to tantrums. It might have been frustration at the treatment he endured at the hands of his counsellors or simply a fault in his personality, but he never seemed to mature into a confident and respected ruler.

It cannot be denied that the terrible effects of the Black Death in 1348 in the early part of his reign would have tested the most hardened and experienced ruler. Other outbreaks occurred but in general terms that of the fourteenth century was the most virulent. The Plague arrived into England from the Continent via black rats from a ship that entered Weymouth. It was transmitted by fleas carried by the vermin. Within hours, victims developed large black lumps or 'buboes' under their arms or in their groins. It seemed to target the glandular areas and after about two days of agony a victim would die. The worst affected were obviously those living in cramped conditions in the towns, although it eventually spread to the countryside. Because it made no distinction, senior religious figures like the Archbishop of Canterbury fell victim. In a superstitious age this caused terror in the minds of the population and led to a questioning of previously accepted values. Within a couple of years between a third and a half of the population had been wiped out. Unfortunately, the Plague coincided with a year of abnormally excessive rainfall, causing rotted crops in the fields and accentuating the misery of the surviving population due to famine.

The social implications quickly began to surface. There were too few workers to harvest those crops which did grow, or to cultivate the fields already in growth. Animals were unattended and the trade at markets halted. On account of the reduced numbers of workmen available, rich landowners began to panic and vie among one another for their services.

In turn the labourers began to realise that these conditions had put them in a position where they could bargain for higher wages. To stop the trend, statutes were issued by the government in support of landowners' rights to impose pay restraint.

There were other undercurrents swirling through the minds of people of all classes at the time, albeit for differing reasons. The peasantry, in spite of religion being dinned into them, were still subject to the superstitions of the age. They had been raised to regard the clergy with a respect amounting to almost awe. When the plague struck the fact that it did not differentiate between the priest and the pauper, no matter how many prayers were said, inclined many to question the power of the Church to keep them safe or even give a believable explanation for the phenomenon. The Church authorities owned about a third of all the land which they worked in exactly the same manner as any other landowner. Labourers realised that the Church as an employer had to be considered in the same light as anyone else in the changing economics engendered by the labour shortage. This caused a great deal of friction.

During this time a movement arose among the adherents of the views expounded by John Wycliffe, regarding the papacy and its agents. In particular, exception was taken to the massive ownership of land by the Church authorities from which they gleaned immense wealth while the bulk of the population lived in abject poverty. The name 'Lollards' ascribed to one group which originated in the Netherlands about the beginning of the fourteenth century was used contemptuously to describe heretical groups and sects of this type.

An attempt by landowners to revive the custom of serfdom and villeinage which, over many years had become practically obsolete, also had an inflammatory effect on the disaffected peasant classes. The shortage of labour caused by the ravages of the Black Death which had killed so many people was a driving force behind the disturbance. For the first time it held out the belief that they could bargain their way to better conditions.

To add to the woes of the labouring classes a further tax (a poll tax) was levied on each person within a parish. The already impoverished people in many parishes falsified their returns by understating the number of inhabitants to reduce the charge on the parish and consequently the contribution of each individual. The deception was discovered and those involved were subjected to such severe punishments that the peasants of Kent, Essex, Cambridgeshire, Norfolk and Suffolk were incited to rebellion. They marched on London in June 1381 led by John Ball a gifted orator and determined agitator for change, and Wat Tyler, a man who had seen action in various wars.

As always with mobs there were some who had different objectives, and who under the cloak of genuine grievances committed violent crimes. Without doubt the atrocities which occurred sullied the cause of those genuinely seeking a lawful remedy to the oppressive conditions under which they lived. To defuse the situation the young king rode among them, listened to their complaints and assured them that they would be corrected if all could be concluded peacefully. The bulk of the rioters accepted these assurances and eventually dispersed. Tyler and his cohorts, however, felt that they were too vague and demanded a more clear-cut solution.

The king agreed to a second meeting, this time at Smithfield, with the leaders of the rebellion, but the demands from Tyler had become more extreme and his manner toward the king more aggressive. At one point, in the belief that Tyler was making a threatening gesture against the king, the mayor, William Walworth, remonstrated with him and in response Tyler aimed a strike at him with a dagger. Walworth retaliated as did one of the king's retainers and Tyler was killed.

In spite of royal assurances that the wrongs would be put right, it was never done and the reprisals against those who had taken part in the uprising were cruel. These actions were in keeping with the rest of Richard's characteristics, which manifested themselves more clearly the longer he reigned: unreliable, unjust and untrustworthy. In fact, he was more of a dictator than a king. In 1389 he dismissed his uncle, the Duke of Gloucester, the council and all its adherents and took over the reins of government himself.

After numerous struggles the English people had gradually teased out of their rulers a great many concessions and over the years had become accustomed to a parliamentary system of government. To have this so dismissively and autocratically called to a halt was an unforgivable affront. All classes – barons, landowners, burgesses and judiciary, not forgetting the important agricultural industry, were outraged. Richard rejected any pleas of mitigation and dealt severely with anyone, regardless of class, who flouted his laws

In 1398 a dispute had broken out between the Duke of Hereford (the son of John of Gaunt) and the Duke of Norfolk, and the king banished them both from the realm. A year later the Duke of Lancaster died, whereupon Richard, instead of exhibiting a measure of real common-sense, confiscated his considerable estates. In doing so he set in train events which would lose him his life and crown, ironically to the very person he had injured. Even more seriously, he set the scene for the beginning of the Wars of the Roses. The Duke of Hereford, or Bolingbroke as he was known, taking advantage of the king's absence in Ireland, landed with a small force on the coast of Yorkshire in 1399 and on 30 September Parliament deposed Richard and awarded the crown to Bolingbroke – Henry of Lancaster, who became Henry IV. On his return to England, Richard was captured and incarcerated in Pontefract Castle in Yorkshire, where he died the following year, 1400, possibly from starvation.

Henry IV

Born in 1367, Henry was the son of John of Gaunt and cousin of the deposed Richard II. Taking the throne in 1399, he made an inauspicious start. His intentions were good and without doubt he was replacing a king who had created discord and chaos throughout the land, but he would be forever saddled with the label 'usurper'. This in itself launched a tainted inheritance which had violent factions bubbling in its wake.

Inevitably, plots began to formulate which in themselves were debilitating both personally and for the country as a whole. One such was uncovered in 1400 and quickly snuffed out. Sensing the uncertainty attending the new king's position, the Scots and their allies and paymasters, the French, pressed what they saw as an advantage. The former, under their leader Archibald Earl of Douglas invaded from the north which was defended by the powerful Percy family under the Earl of Northumberland (Hotspur), whose stronghold at Alnwick dominated the border region. The two armies met at Homildon Hill, near Wooler, in 1402 and the Scots were decisively defeated. The Earl of Douglas and almost 100 of his nobles were taken prisoner.

Because the Percies were acting on behalf of the crown they felt that the cost of prosecuting the conflict should be borne by the sovereign and petitioned to be compensated accordingly. Henry rejected the request which then raised another cause for strife. Normally the leader of an army and other important members, if captured, were the property of the king for the purpose of ransom. On this occasion Hotspur, having funded the operation, held the view that since the king was not paying for any of the costs of the battle the revenue for the prisoners was his as partial compensation for the operation. Naturally, a quarrel was the result. The Percies were aggrieved because they had been staunch supporters of Henry against Richard, and without their assistance he might not have gained the throne. Matters boiled up to a pitch where resentment led to actions bordering on recklessness. First the Percies, in a fit of defiance, decided to release Douglas under a treaty. Secondly, they conspired with Owen Glendower, a formidable man who had emerged as the Welsh leader, to join forces to unseat the king

The plan was to meet at Shrewsbury to face the king's army in the field. The king, however, made a forced march and arrived a number of hours earlier than expected, which was a disaster for the Percies because the battle took place before the arrival of Glendower's forces. That they did not take part substantially weakened the army of the Percies and they were defeated, Hotspur was killed, his uncle taken prisoner and subsequently beheaded. Other than that, Henry dealt with most of the remaining members of the dissidents relatively compassionately, and one senior figure, the Earl of Northumberland, was pardoned. Three years later another insurrection broke out, this time led by the Earl of Nottingham in league with Scrope, Archbishop of York. This too was put down. In the same year, 1405, a ship on its way to France was intercepted with James, son and heir to Robert, king of Scotland on board. He was taken prisoner and detained in England. The remaining years of Henry's reign were fairly uneventful. He died in 1413 whereupon his son, Henry V, became king.

Owen Glendower

An erudite man, Glendower was studying in London for the Bar when he came to the notice of Richard II who engaged him as an equerry. As a consequence he became a staunch supporter of the king. After Richard

---

was deposed he returned to Wales, gathered together an army and headed an insurrection against Henry's rule in Wales, with some success. He conducted a type of guerrilla war against Henry's Marcher lords, disappearing into the fastnesses of mountain regions after an engagement. His tactics were successful enough to entice Henry to negotiate terms, but before he was able to engage in them Glendower died.

Henry V

Born at Monmouth in 1387, Henry is reputed to have been somewhat undisciplined as a youth. Upon ascending the throne in 1413 he soon shed his previous attitudes and was regarded as a wise and thoughtful ruler in most respects. By the time he took over the crown he was thoroughly practiced in the arts of war, experience of which he gained while supporting his father in various conflicts.

Probably out of the sheer practicality of securing the borders with Scotland he restored to the Percies their estates in Northumberland and set free the Earl of March after a short but abortive rising. Another possible reason was a decision to revive the claim for the French crown. After observing the continuing conflict between the Dukes of Orleans and Burgundy Henry decided that this was a propitious moment to take advantage of the turbulent situation and landed a force near Harfleur.

The castle there was strongly defended and robust, and was won at great cost in fighting men which was very damaging to Henry's cause. Perhaps the most serious losses were because of sickness. This, it is believed, was brought about by the water they had been using, while encamped outside the town, being contaminated. Large numbers were affected by dysentery and a substantial number were transported back to England by ship.

Henry decided to call off the expedition and take the remainder of his small force back to England via Calais. During the march eastwards the rain fell incessantly and although it made the journey difficult, and the fording of swollen rivers extremely hazardous, it held a hidden and unexpected benefit later on.

They were confronted by a large and well equipped French army intending to block their way and bring them to battle. For obvious reasons Henry tried to avoid what appeared to be an unequal contest and asked merely to be allowed to leave France, but the French, with their overwhelming superiority of numbers, would have none of it and the battle finally took place at a place called Agincourt on 25 October 1415.

The French chose the place of battle to suit the large numbers of cavalry which they intended to employ. The terrain was open ground flanked by dense woodlands, which meant that Henry had to work out a strategy to nullify their advantage. He noticed that the incessant rain had made the ground soggy and therefore he drew his force back as far as possible, realising that heavy cavalry would labour under such conditions. He also made his men cut pointed stakes and plant them into the ground as a defence against the knights. These tactics worked so well that the French knights were slowed down before they were halfway to the English lines, but were within range of the English and Welsh archers at the barriers, who then proceeded to launch a devastating flight of arrows, causing appalling casualties. Those who did reach the English lines were already in an exhausted state and were either killed or captured for ransom. The French then tried to retreat but became entangled with another line of attackers being ordered forward. The confusion resulted in more being slaughtered by the archers and foot soldiers.

Against all the odds, the flower of French chivalry and their glittering and massive army were utterly defeated.

Among the dead such was the number of high ranking nobles of the French aristocracy that for many years to come they were almost bereft of suitable leaders to counter either a successful invasion by the young king of England or intervene in the civil war between the Dukes of Burgundy and Orleans, which was tearing France apart. The following year, 1416, to compound French misery, they were defeated at sea by a fleet under the Duke of Bedford.

Henry returned to Normandy with a substantial army in 1417 to consolidate and expand on his previous victory. His progress was such that the young Duke of Burgundy, whose father had just been assassinated, joined forces with him, forming a powerful alliance. This brought about the Treaty of Troyes (21 May 1420) which contained some remarkably far-reaching concessions. The first was betrothal of Catherine, the daughter of the French king, to Henry, and another was that Charles VI would retain the throne of France until his death whereupon Henry and his heirs would inherit it.

The son of Charles VI (known as the Dauphin) was naturally infuriated at losing his inheritance, so while Henry and his bride were back in England he gathered his supporters to contest the terms agreed at Troyes. Henry's brother, the Duke of Clarence, who had remained in Normandy, probably in the role of caretaker, bore the brunt of the Dauphin's resentment when he was attacked and defeated by the French in coalition with a large Scottish army, the joint forces being led by the Earl of Buchan. This induced Henry to return with an army, first to secure Normandy and then to make other gains. This astonishing young man once more eliminated a powerful French army and that of their Scottish allies, finally entering Paris as the dominating force in the whole of France. Thereafter, the Scots were unable to raise such an army to reinforce their allies.

Henry's achievements were immense. He was the king of England, soon to be king of France. He was married to Catherine, the beautiful daughter of the king of France who had recently borne a son to continue the line. What more could he wish for? Life was indeed sweet! Unfortunately, while he was at Vincennes, just outside Paris, he contracted the dreaded dysentery and at the early age of just 35 and at the height of his powers he suddenly died in 1422. The final irony was that barely two months later Charles VI also died. But for that small margin of time and this sequence of events Henry would have become the undisputed king of France and, altering substantially the course of European history forever.

The only serious blot on the otherwise impeccable career of Henry V was his persecution of the Lollards. This he engaged in, rather cynically, to gain the support of the clergy who were then more willing to subscribe funds to bolster his military activities.

There was, however, a circumstance which would manifest itself in the following reign and bring serious repercussions in its train. This was the inherent insanity suffered by Charles VII of France and further transmitted by Catherine to their son Henry VI. It would eventually emerge to cast a shadow over his reign.

At this juncture it would be unjust not to mention the fortitude and contribution of Welsh archers in the victory of Agincourt. By this time the soldiers of both countries were often a united force possessed of incredible skill with the bow and in this battle they proved to be an irresistible combination.

Henry VI

England entered another tricky period where a young child inherited the throne at the age of 9 months and the country was governed once again by committee, consisting of uncles and cousins, with disastrous consequences. The Dukes of Gloucester and Bedford were in overall charge including that of Henry's care, tuition and general instruction to prepare him for his eventual succession.

Within a matter of weeks he also became, on the death of his grandfather Charles VI of France, the king of France in accordance with the terms of the Treaty of Troyes. He was crowned king of England at Westminster in 1429 and king of France at Paris in 1430. When he reached maturity he was always a gentle soul whose piety impeded his ability to fulfil his obligations as a ruler.

The Dauphin, however, still smarting from the events which had robbed him of the throne, enlisted many supporters to his cause, especially those who had most to gain from his success, and they began to attack all the territories in France held by the English. At first they fared rather badly until the intervention of a young peasant girl named Joan of Arc (Jeanne d'Arc) the Maid of Orleans. This remarkable young visionary claimed that she had heard angelic voices which instructed her to present herself to the Dauphin, and convince him that she had been divinely chosen to lead the army in a campaign to overthrow the English, this at a time when the Dauphin was becoming resigned to controlling only some southern provinces of France. She succeeded in persuading him that she was not insane and that her motives were simply to regain France and have him installed as king. Furthermore, she somehow convinced him that she was fully capable of achieving this by force of arms.

The fact is that that she did lead the French armies, amazingly taking precedence over battle-hardened generals and even more impressively frequently leading those armies to success. Against almost all belief she assisted the Dauphin to realise his ambition to become king and was at his side in Rheims Cathedral during his coronation.

Eventually she was taken prisoner by the Burgundian troops

who sold her to the English, who in turn were obliged to hand her over to the Church authorities who had branded her a sorceress. Put on trial as such, her revelations were declared to be the work of Satan and she was condemned to death. The punishment was commuted to life imprisonment but, almost a year to the day later, she faced trial again. This time it was stated that she remained unrepentant and again invoked sacrilegious acts. She was convicted and placed under the penalty of death by being burned at the stake. This was done at Orleans on 30 May 1431. She died with the same bravery evident throughout her life.

Had she never existed and some modern-day novelist had written a book of a peasant girl in the fifteenth century purporting to have accomplished such astonishing feats it would have been treated with utmost derision, especially if the story had ended as it did almost 300 years later when she was canonised at St Peter's in Rome. No, she was not English, and I started by stating that this was the 'English legacy', but she had so profound an influence on the history of both England and France that it would have been unthinkable to ignore a life which throbbed with such inspiration and fervour.

The English were still a substantial presence in France but their strength was sapped by further reverses of fortune. First the Duke of Bedford, who was acting as regent of France, died, thereby removing a powerful leader, and as the military tide began to favour the French, the Duke of Burgundy, realising that his bread might be buttered more tastily elsewhere, defected to the French side. The transfer of alliance of this powerful figure changed the balance of power to such a degree that by 1453 Charles VII had consolidated his hold on the whole of France with the exception of Calais.

On the heels of the collapse of the English presence in France followed an equally disastrous failure of administrative policy at home, mainly due to the inadequacy of the pious but weak Henry VI. Unfortunately he was another rather saintly king, more suited to the priesthood than to the role of a monarch of the time. This required characteristics such as forcefulness and organising ability combined with a certain amount of ruthlessness to counteract the grasping and self-seeking approach of the nobility who had been weaned on a diet of warfare and plunder in France. The baronial class, being deprived of a source of profit since the loss of French territories, turned their attention to improving their fortunes in England. This meant attaching their loyalties, sometimes only temporarily, to the side which they believed most likely to succeed. After all, these barons had at their disposal fully trained troops most of whom had experienced action on the Continent, and if deployed for the service from which they might derive the most benefit, may be crucial to the right bidder. A perfect example of this was the Earl of Warwick (Richard Neville) who exploited this technique to such an extent that he became known as the 'kingmaker'.

Hostilities commenced between the Houses of York and Lancaster, eventually turning into what became a civil war, known as the Wars of the Roses. They had their roots in the alleged usurpation by Henry IV of the throne then held by his cousin Richard II. Admittedly Richard had been something of a tyrant and had brought chaos to the country, nevertheless his close and powerful family members could not bring themselves to accept what they regarded as an illegal infringement of the succession and their resentment was still smouldering.

The legal title to the throne strictly on the grounds of primogeniture, it was argued, belonged to the Duke of York who was, by general agreement, occupying the position of chief minister and protector. He was seemingly quite content for this arrangement to continue until an action which smacked of outright antagonism by Margaret of Anjou, whom Henry had married in 1445. Margaret was aggressive and strong-minded whereas Henry was weak and vacillating. She took advantage of his weak character to virtually dominate future proceedings. She saw York as an ever-present threat to the accession of her own son and chose to remove him from his high position, replacing him with the Earl of Suffolk. It was an ill-conceived move by Margaret who obviously did not have either the imagination or sensitivity to assess the possible outcome of her actions. Unsurprisingly it was seen as inflammatory and a slap in the face for the House of York, and as such was unlikely to go unchallenged. The folly of this appointment was compounded by the total inability of Suffolk to oversee an office of such magnitude, and he was later murdered by someone utterly outraged by his behaviour.

To further complicate matters it was becoming apparent that Henry's mental grasp of life was not quite complete and far from that which was essential to a mediaeval king. This was due to the fact that he had inherited from his maternal grandfather, the French King Charles VI, a form of mental illness which would surface from time to time to render him incapable of rational behaviour.

It is doubtful if there was ever a more confusing sequence of events in our history. I am not normally an enthusiast of the simple presentation of statistics but on this occasion, without at least a few of them, it is difficult to unravel the plot. Battles, dates and place names have been included together with names of some of the major participants to help clarify matters.

It was primarily a family feud among the descendants of Edward III who were contesting the right to inherit the throne. Quite simply, two of his sons, one the Duke of Lancaster and the other the Duke of York, and their descendants, plus Henry's wife, Margaret of Anjou, who played a pivotal part, were among the principal characters in the dispute. Although it lasted for generations the general population was largely unaffected. The principal exceptions were excesses permitted by Margaret when she callously allowed the sacking of Ludlow and Newbury, and the pillaging of the countryside by her mercenaries after the second Battle of St Albans. This was because the battles were fought by the supporters of the royal contestants who were also substantial landowners; they depended on their lands to produce the revenue to support their armies as well as to maintain their standard of living, so they made sure that those same lands were not devastated. The battles were sporadic rather than continuous, with power switching from one to the other as each gained a temporary advantage and both parties strove throughout to garner the approval of both Parliament and the population. By doing so they would ensure that final success would make for a seamless assumption of power. Nevertheless they were vicious and bloody battles with great loss of life.

Margaret of Anjou

Margaret of Anjou was born in 1430 and died in 1482. She was a competent commander of troops with a good grasp of strategy, albeit somewhat ruthless. A manipulative operator, she inveigled many of the northerners over to her side and also conspired with the Scots and their French allies. At the conclusion of the conflict she was imprisoned for four years before being released to return to France in response to a ransom of 50,000 crowns paid by Louis XI.

Richard Neville, Earl of Warwick (the 'kingmaker')

Neville was born in 1428 and was killed at the Battle of Barnet in 1471. He was a strong supporter of and adviser to Edward IV, and played a part in the Yorkists' victory at St Albans in 1455, although his father, the Earl of Salisbury, was the main strategist of that victory. At the end of the year he fought at Wakefield when the Yorkists suffered a defeat and his father and the Duke of York were killed.

In 1464 after the Battle of Hexham a rift developed between Warwick and Edward. Warwick had been despatched to France to broker a marriage between Edward and the sister of the French king, but while he was away Edward secretly married the widow of Sir John Grey. It can only be presumed that the diversion was calculated because he knew in advance that Warwick was opposed to the union and would have tried to prevent it. The upshot was that Warwick was so alienated by such duplicity that he transferred his allegiance to Henry VI and Margaret. He also conspired with Edward's brother George, Duke of Clarence, against Edward.

Edward IV

Edward was born in 1442 and died in 1483. He reigned from 1461 to 1470, when he was ousted, and then from 1471 to 1483. He married Elizabeth Woodville secretly in 1464.

Subsequent to the Battle of Wakefield, where his father was killed, Edward assumed the crown but it was only after the Yorkists had won the desperate battle against the odds just over a month later at Mortimers Cross in 1461 that he entered London and was recognised by popular acclaim, Henry being deposed. At this battle he showed his outstanding tactical ability. A couple of months later Edward faced another army under Margaret, packed with mercenaries from France, Scotland, Ireland, Brittany and miscellaneous Continental levies. This was the Battle of Towton, said to be one of the bloodiest battles ever to take place on English soil.

At approximately this time, Edward embarked on his imprudent marriage to a widow who had two sons already, thus offending his uncle, the Earl of Warwick, and his brother George, Duke of Clarence, who had been his staunchest supporters. They went over to the Lancastrian side, and then, together with other powerful allies, raised an army, forcing Edward to seek safety on the Continent. Poor old Henry was restored to the throne by these puppeteers – not that he was fully aware by this time of what was going on around him. In the interim Edward had been supplied with a small force by the Duke of Burgundy which he led ashore at Ravenspur in Yorkshire. He was rapidly joined by a large following of partisans which marched swiftly to London and quickly deposed and imprisoned Henry. The country was again in a state of flux. Two battles were fought in fairly quick succession (Barnet, where Warwick was killed, and Tewkesbury, where Henry's son Edward, Prince of Wales, lost his life). Henry and Margaret were both subsequently incarcerated.

George, Duke of Clarence, was forgiven and restored to his estates, but proved to be a serial conspirator who could not accept any restriction of his conduct. After a member of his household had been condemned by the king for a serious offence, Clarence took it upon himself to countermand the execution of the sentence – as a result, he was impeached by the king, condemned in 1478, and consigned to the Tower where he was killed. Legend has it that he was drowned in a butt of Malmsey wine.

From then until he died, Edward's reign, at least in England, was relatively peaceful. He did try to revive the claim to the French throne and invaded France. Whether this was a genuine attempt or a means of keeping the turbulent nobles too busy to create mischief at home we will never know, but in 1475 Louis XI concluded an arrangement to pay him 75,000 crowns down and 20,000 crowns per annum to leave France and not return.

5

The Wars of the Roses

This was the beginning of a dramatic period in England's history and the leading players in the next phase were:

Henry VI (of the House of Lancaster), married Margaret of Anjou 1445.

Humphrey of Gloucester, son of Henry IV, murdered 1447, it is believed on the orders of Margaret.

Henry VI suffered a period of insanity during 1453–54.

Duke of York appointed Protector once more by Parliament in 1453.

Edward, Prince of Wales, born to Henry IV and Margaret in 1453 after nine years of marriage. Doubts were cast on parentage.

Earl of Suffolk. Margaret replaced Duke of York as Protector in favour of the Earl of Suffolk. The latter was the person who had gone to France to broker her marriage to Henry VI. He then became her confidant. Apart from introducing punitive taxes, he was suspected by many in the military of treachery and intrigue with France. This is believed to be the reason for his murder.

Duke of York raised an army on 22 May 1455 and marched

on London. Defeated the King at the first Battle of St Albans. Henry was captured but released.

Henry VI became mentally ill in 1454. The Duke of York resumed the position of Regent and Lord Protector until 1455 when the king had recovered sufficiently to return to court. York was then ousted from the Regency at the instigation of Margaret and banned from State affairs.

Duke of York reinstated as Protector.

Four years of peace ensued, or at least without conflict, while Margaret campaigned for support.

BATTLES BETWEEN THE HOUSES OF LANCASTER AND YORK

1st battle of St Albans, 2 May 1455. The architect of the resounding victory for the Yorkist party was undoubtedly the Earl of Warwick.

Bloreheath, 3 September 1459. Led by the Duke of York and the Earl of Salisbury, they again defeated the Lancastrians.

Ludford Bridge, 12 October 1459. It never materialised into a battle. It became more of a confrontation as a result of Margaret's emissaries being sent to the Yorkist commanders with an offer of a full pardon for any of their adherents willing to rescind allegiance to the Yorkist cause. This created an atmosphere of uncertainty in their ranks which, it has been suggested, persuaded the Yorkist leaders to leave the field without offering battle in case the waverers decided to take the offer.

Northampton, 10 July 1460. The Lancastrians were defeated by the Yorkists who were once again led by the redoubtable 'Earl of Warwick' the son of the Earl of Salisbury.

Wakefield, 30 December 1460. Henry V forces won and the Duke of York killed.

Mortimer's Cross, 2 February 1461. Yorkists won led by Edward IV himself.

2nd battle of St Albans, 17 February 1461. Lancastrians won – personally led by Margaret (Henry V I released).

Towton, 29 March 1461. Won by Edward IV, son of the Duke of York.

Hedgeley Moor, 25 April 1464. Yorkists prevailed once more.

Hexham, 15 May 1464. Yorkists victorious, led by Montague.

Edgecote Moor, 26 July 1469. Lancastrians victorious.

Losecoat Field, 12 March 1470. A fairly minor battle which the Yorkists won.

Henry VI. Restored to throne in 1470 by the Earl of Warwick (King maker) who was now fighting for Margaret and the Lancastrians.

Barnet, 14 April 1471. Yorkists won – Warwick killed (Edward reinstated).

Tewkesbury, 4 May 1471. Yorkists maintained their advantage, Henry died a few days after the battle (murdered/executed?). Differing opinions may be advanced on this episode but in some aspects there is an impression that it heralded the decline of feudalism and a gradual enhancement of Parlimentary influence.

Significant Events of the Period

Academic institutions

Henry VI founded Eton College in 1440 and King's College Cambridge in 1441. Margaret of Anjou founded Queens' College Cambridge in 1448. Queens' is so spelt because it was allegedly founded again in 1465 by Elizabeth, the queen of Edward IV, although how something can be founded by two different people 17 years apart is difficult to comprehend.

Jack Cade

Cade led a middle-class insurrection in 1450 protesting against bad government and corruption. It was not a revolt of the peasantry as in 1381 but of people of more substance. They met and defeated, near Sevenoaks, Kent, a royal force sent against them. Continuing their rebellion they then marched on London which they occupied for a couple of days. A promise of pardon and other assurances were given and the rebels dispersed. Cade as the instigator was held responsible for some violent atrocities in London by errant members of his followers. He was pursued as far as Heathfield in Sussex where he was killed. A pub there still bears his name.

William Caxton

In 1476 Caxton, who had been an influential figure in the commercial circles of Bruges, learned the newly-developed art of printing and brought it back to England. More details of this man's achievements and influence on written English can be found in the chapter dedicated to those who influenced English life.

Sir Thomas Malory

Sir Thomas was the author of a book, *Le Morte D'Arthur*, which was a compilation of stories about King Arthur and his Knights of the Round Table, printed by Caxton about 1470. It was immensely popular and led to a flood of speculation about the exact location of Camelot.

The Resumption of Dissent

With the death of Henry VI and the unopposed accession of Edward IV it could have been assumed that the Wars of the Roses were at an end. This should have been the case but Edward paid the price for his gluttony and moral laxity by suddenly dying at the age of 41 leaving two sons, Edward and Richard, both of whom were minors. The older brother Edward was the natural successor to the throne as Edward V. His brother Richard held the title of Duke of York. Their uncle, the Duke of Gloucester, the brother of the recently deceased king was declared Lord Protector of the Realm and he duly caused his nephew, the young Edward V, to be declared king. In the course of this ceremony, as was required, Gloucester solemnly took the oath of fealty.

Edward V, born 1470. Crowned 1483, reigned for only 2 months.

Richard III, born 1452 (another usurper). Ascended the throne 1483.

Within a matter of months, Richard, after declaring his loyalty to his nephew, the young King Edward, as the rightful heir to the throne, obviously reconsidered the situation. Suddenly he had Edward and his younger brother Richard conveyed to the Tower where they were incarcerated without charge or explanation. In fact little or no information seems to have been offered. It was inferred that it was to protect them while in their minority but the secrecy led to rumours which were damaging to the Duke of Gloucester's reputation, a situation which was used to the full extent by his opponents. On the other hand it might have been true that Richard had decided to put them out of the way, hoping that when they reached their majority they could be shown to be unfit for the task of sovereignty. Whatever the reason the occasion never arose because, after being placed in captivity, they disappeared. The presumption, and that it all that is left to history, is that they were murdered. There is the possibility that other claimants to the accession might have been involved. Shakespeare's view was clearly that Richard was the guilty party as the obvious beneficiary. This play was written long after the event, however. Richard was apparently a decisive man who rarely conferred with even his closest advisors before taking action. He executed, without trial, Lord Hastings and Earl Rivers, which made the alarm bells ring for many, especially as Hastings had been his close friend. This enabled the Woodvilles and Beauforts to subject him to an acrimonious propaganda campaign with far-reaching effects.

There was one claimant to the succession who now came into the reckoning and with some support – Henry of Richmond. He was, through the female line, a descendant of John of Gaunt from his illicit relationship with his mistress Katherine Swynford. On the other side, he was the grandson of Owen Tudor who had married the widow of Henry V.

None of this could put a royal hallmark on his lineage but he was considered to be as near to royalty as could reasonably be produced. For a number of years he had been allowed to live in exile under the protection of the Duke of Brittany. It was from there with a small force of about 2,000 men, consisting of both Yorkist and Lancastrian veterans, that he launched his invasion, landing at Milford Haven on 7 August 1485. Joined by several thousand more he met Richard's army at Market Bosworth in Leicestershire on 22 August. Richard was killed at the battle and Richmond became Henry VII.

The marriage in 1486 between Henry VII and Elizabeth of York joined together the Houses of Lancaster and York into what was an almost romantically scripted conclusion to the Wars of the Roses.

6

The Tudors

Henry VII

Henry was the first Tudor king, having been born in 1457 and taken the crown in 1485. He reigned for 12 years and died in 1509. He married Elizabeth of York in 1486.

It was fortunate that the new king was an accomplished administrator for, on his accession, the country was in considerable disorder. Henry observed that the protracted Wars of the Roses had demonstrated clearly that the baronial classes, through their attachment to feudal practices, would continue to be a perennially disrupting influence, unless curbed. He set about reducing their wealth and influence by punitive taxes and fines for insubordination. Commerce was encouraged to the benefit of country and treasury alike. By strong and wise government Henry managed to create stability in a nation so long at war with itself. Obviously his marriage to Elizabeth of York united the Houses of Lancaster and York and provided a more solid foundation for the country.

More than his predecessors Henry looked further than France to make alliances through marriage, and brought about a match between his eldest son Arthur and Catherine, the daughter of King Ferdinand V of Aragon and Isabella of Castile. Ferdinand, by marrying Isabella of Castile, had unified two important regions of Spain and formed the basis for a unified Spain. He led the country against the occupying Moors and after 10 years of bloody fighting conquered Granada. He was definitely an ally worth keeping. The marriage took place in 1501 but Arthur died suddenly in 1502 after only a few months of wedlock.

Apart from the shock of losing a son there were other implications of major importance. The tragedy had also ruptured a budding alliance with a very powerful European monarchy. Another matter arose which, although of lesser importance, had delicate overtones which needed careful and refined diplomacy to address successfully. This had regard to the terms and conditions of the marriage now ended by Arthur's untimely death.

The eminence of Catherine's parents meant that the dowry which was to accompany her marriage was lavish. It was also conditional upon the bridegroom being enthroned at the time of payment being completed. This posed a problem for the avaricious and somewhat impoverished Henry because it meant that the first part would have to be returned to her father King Ferdinand and the remainder forfeited.

This was when Henry's skill as a manipulative negotiator was shown to full effect. He probably concluded that should he be able to bring about a marriage between his second son, Henry, and the widow of Arthur, the situation might be saved. He would be able, no doubt, to point out to young Henry the overall economic advantages and the dangers of not complying with the plan. By careful, sensitive and respectful reasoning with Catharine it could be shown that for her to return to her homeland as a young widow may not guarantee her future happiness.

If she married the handsome, vigorous young Henry, with whom she was already well acquainted, she would in time become queen. After all, the original purpose behind the arranged marriage between her and Arthur was to forge a link between the two countries. Subsequent events suggest that Catherine was quite happy within the environment of the English court which made her more than merely acquiescent to the arrangement.

Having established the wishes and agreement of Catherine and the young Henry, success now depended on gaining the agreement of King Ferdinand and influencing the Pope to give his dispensation to the proposed wedding. Ultimately, Henry achieved all of his objectives: Catherine and the young Henry were betrothed on the understanding that they would marry when he reached 18 years of age. King Henry retained the dowry, and the marriage took place seven years later, in 1509.

Two actions by Henry VII carried incalculable portents for the future. First, as things turned out, during the next reign, the marriage described above was used by his son as a vehicle to pursue other ambitions, and effectively altered England's religious orientation. Second, his eldest daughter married James IV of Scotland, the consequences of which, after the death of Elizabeth, culminated in the union of the crowns of England and Scotland in 1603.

During his reign there were unsuccessful uprisings led by Lord Lovel and the Staffords in 1486. There were also two impostures named Lambert Simnel (1487) and Perkin Warbeck (1496–1499). The former was trained to impersonate the son of the Duke of Clarence (of Malmsey wine butt notoriety). Crowned in Dublin his army of insurgents were defeated at Newark on 16 June 1487. This simpleton who was merely a pawn in the game was forgiven and ended up as a kitchen skivvy. The latter was put forward by Margaret of York as a pretender to the throne against Henry. She claimed he was her nephew, Richard Plantagenet, the younger of the two princes who were murdered in the Tower. He married a kinswoman of the Scottish King James IV. The French and their allies, the Scots, recognised an opportunity and supported his cause, but after several abortive attempts at invasion he was finally captured and executed in 1499.

By restricting the power of the warlike and autocratic baronial classes, Henry VII unwittingly, or perhaps deliberately, gave impetus to the rise of the middle classes with their commercial acumen. They formed the thinking layer of society as far as the making and application of the law was concerned and also promoted the benefits of peaceful trade and prosperity. Increased revenue accrued, which in turn provided another lucrative source of tax. As a byproduct of their increasing importance the collective parliamentary voice of this newly empowered layer of society carried more resonance. Henry's astute manipulation of the various layers of society was seen by the way that he elevated the role of the middle ranks while at the same time depressing the feudal nobility; the net result was a strengthening of the crown.

Henry showed far-sightedness when he encouraged exploration outside the confines of Europe. In 1496 he gave a commission to John Cabot, a Venetian pilot and an expert navigator, and his sons, to undertake a voyage of discovery of lands then unknown. Cabot, frustrated at being unable to obtain patronage from other countries, had been resident in England from time to time since 1472. After being charged with this instruction he successfully landed at places later named Nova Scotia and Cape Breton Island, and also landed on the mainland of North America. His son Sebastian led a later voyage visiting Labrador and Newfoundland.

The king left a lasting memorial to his reign by building the Henry VII chapel at Westminster, and on a lighter note, playing cards became popular during his reign. A portrait of his queen, Elizabeth of York, has appeared eight times in every pack of cards for the last 500 years. Claims that playing cards were invented in England are disputed by some scholars who think they may have been used in ancient Egypt.

Henry VIII

Henry VIII was born in 1491, ascended to the throne in 1509 and reigned for 38 years. The fact that he had six wives in the space of about ten years is perhaps the over-riding memory of his reign.

All the chroniclers speak of Henry at the time of his succession as being a man of high intelligence, handsome, with a fine physique and the energy to combine these features to good effect. He was interested in music and learning which extended into theology, which he studied assiduously. His writings on the subject, in which he refuted the teachings of Martin Luther, received praise from the Pope who rewarded him with the title 'Defender of the Faith'.

In spite of the fact that his father had concluded a peace with France, Henry decided, without preamble, to invade that country. Landing at Calais with about 25,000 men in 1513 he was met by a French army which apparently had little enthusiasm for the fray, because their knights beat a hasty retreat from the field causing the conflict to be named derisively 'The Battle of the Spurs'. The only semblance of success from this campaign was the taking of Tournai, which had no lasting benefit.

During his absence the Scots, supported by their French allies, decided upon a large invasion, based on the belief that, as England's army was engaged in France, their defences would be too weak to withstand an attack from the north. A hurriedly conscripted army under the Earl of Surrey was assembled and met them at Flodden Field, Northumberland, on 9 September 1513. The result was a defeat for the Scots in which they lost their king, James IV, the Archbishop of St Andrews, the flower of their nobility, as well as about 12,000 men. There is a memorial to the tragic day on the site of the battle which can be reached by leaving the A1 just north of Morpeth and following the A697 towards

Branxton. Queen Margaret, the widow of James IV, was also the sister of Henry VIII and this was possibly the reason she was granted peace without the usual harsh treatment meted out to a defeated enemy.

Most descriptions of Henry's life centre on his numerous marriages and the notorious manner in which some of them ended. It is worth a glance at some of the background causes which prompted his behaviour. Henry's first wife, Catherine of Aragon, had been married to him for 18 years before any signs of estrangement were seen. She was six years his senior, making her at the time of the divorce attempt about 42 years of age. All of the children she had borne, with the exception of Mary, had died in infancy so it was hardly feasible to expect her to be able to produce a son and heir at her time of life. A legitimate son and heir was Henry's consuming passion to secure the succession, so he decided to try to end the marriage. There was the obvious obstacle of permission from the Pope. Catherine had led a chaste and blameless life which obviated some of the more basic excuses for Henry to employ. Her staunch belief in the sanctity of marriage prompted her to resist attempts to persuade her to comply with his request of annulment. Henry expelled her from court in 1527 and she went into retirement.

He wanted to marry the young Anne Boleyn, therefore Cardinal Wolsey was instructed to find a way for Henry to convince the Pope of the justice of his request to allow him to put Catherine aside, even against her wish. The argument used was that because Catherine had previously been married to Henry's brother, he had unwittingly entered into an incestuous marriage in the first place. After two years of deliberation his request was thrown out by Rome as being unlawful.

Henry finally repudiated the authority of the Pope over the English Church and declared himself 'Protector and Supreme Head of the Church and Clergy of England'. At the same time he declared Wolsey uncooperative and procrastinating, removed him from office and henceforth relied on Thomas Cranmer. He then declared his marriage to Catherine null and void, whereas his marriage to Anne Boleyn he proclaimed as being entirely lawful.

In 1536 Henry began the dissolution of the monasteries and confiscated their lands and properties. He almost overnight became a tyrant capable of destroying anyone who did not unreservedly accept his actions. Eminent churchmen like John Fisher, Bishop of Rochester, later appointed cardinal by Pope Paul III, was among those to suffer. As representative of the Roman Church he opposed the royal supremacy claimed by Henry, which led to his execution. Thomas More, a distinguished and immensely capable diplomat and lawyer, who had acted loyally on Henry's behalf for a number of years, felt unable to sign the Oath of Supremacy and was summarily executed. These were the better known dignitaries Henry ordered to be despatched; there were hundreds more.

January 1536 saw a number of coincidences. Anne Boleyn suffered a miscarriage of the child she was carrying, frustrating the hopes of Henry once again. Catherine of Aragon, his legal wife (in the eyes of Catholic European law), died, thereby making him a widower. Anne, who apparently had a tempestuous and imperious nature, had not been the submissive wife he had expected and that, combined with a failure to produce an heir, gave him an excuse to be rid of her. After producing or perhaps fabricating evidence of adultery and witchcraft against her, she was taken to the Tower in May of that year and executed.

In the same year Henry married Jane Seymour, who did produce a son (Edward, in 1537), but she died shortly after giving birth.

The next wife, Anne of Cleves, a German princess, followed in 1540. Hans Holbein, a gifted portrait painter, was commissioned by Henry to go to the Continent to paint her portrait. On the evidence of this, Henry proposed to her and they eventually married. It appeared that Holbein from either chivalry or artistic licence had embellished Anne's charms because she was not to Henry's taste and he likened her to a 'Flanders mare'. Compounding this with an inability or unwillingness to learn to speak English she was dowdy in dress, dull and without any interest in music or art of any kind. In this case annulment was the chosen solution. It was negotiated with her agreement which entailed a lavish financial arrangement and that she remain in England. Her period as queen ended after a few months.

In her wake came Catherine Howard who, in complete contrast to her predecessor, was a real beauty with a captivating vivaciousness of manner. She was only 18 years of age which made her more likely to fulfil what Henry now regarded as her obligation – to give him a son. Unfortunately it came to light that this young lady had regarded her virtue rather lightly and one of those with whom she had been linked, rather foolishly speaking out of turn, used words which were later repeated to discredit her. Her fatal miscalculation was that immediately after her marriage she appointed her previous music teacher, Derham, as her private secretary. His was the name most prominent among those with whom she was reputed to have had an affair. She was charged in 1541 with adultery. Her paramours Derham and Culpepper were beheaded and she shared the same fate two months later.

Henry's final marriage was to Catherine Parr who survived him.

In his later years Henry became a tyrant who was profligate with the well managed treasury left to him by his father. He held lavish displays and engaged in pointless and expensive campaigns in France. Scotland and France revived their alliance and James V of Scotland tried again to invade England in 1542, but was defeated at the Battle of Solway

Moss. Henry also displayed a natural violence, which increased as time progressed, even toward his oldest friends, possibly exacerbated by the diseased state of his body.

On the plus side he did plan and build a substantial navy; the first to be constructed in time of peace solely for the protection of our shores and one which challenged the maritime supremacy of the Spanish. This proved to be a prescient decision when it comfortably resisted an attempted invasion by Francis I of France. It also had far-reaching consequences for the Armada. Henry had the Chatham dockyard constructed and also founded Trinity House in 1514, a society for the promotion of commerce and navigation by licensing and regulating pilots and erecting and ordering lighthouses, beacons, buoys etc.

Edward VI

There is not a great deal to say about this rather tragic young man, son of Jane Seymour, who was born in 1537 and died in 1553. He was only a child when he inherited the throne, another under-aged monarch under the influence of senior ministers. When he was 16 he contracted tuberculosis which consumed him rapidly. While on his deathbed he was persuaded by the Duke of Northumberland to name Lady Jane Grey, a Protestant, as his successor, rather than Mary, who had been brought up by her mother Catherine of Aragon in the Catholic faith in defiance of Henry VIII. Northumberland calculated this would ensure his continued regency and running of the country.

Edward, to his great credit for one so young, founded Christ's Hospital (generally known as Blue Coat School), a school in London for supporting and educating poor children. The boys' school was removed from Newgate Street to Horsham in 1902 where it still remains. Among former distinguished pupils were Lamb and Coleridge. He also ordered it to be compulsory for church services to be conducted in English rather than Latin.

Lady Jane Grey

Lady Jane, born in 1537, was queen for only nine days, and died in 1554. As an exercise in intrigue, the actions of the regent, the Duke of Northumberland, in trying to supplant the rightful claims of Mary Tudor in favour of Lady Jane Grey were frankly ludicrous. According to accounts of the time Jane was a highly educated, even learned, girl of considerable beauty. She leavened these attributes, however, with common sense and rebutted the suggestion that she should be the chosen successor to Edward.

Northumberland used his power and also that of the Privy Council to convince her that 'it was God's will' and if she refused it would be to the detriment of the country and reverse the Reformation brought about by Henry VIII. It should be remembered that she was also his daughter-in-law. They then proclaimed her 'queen' and as a precaution sought to take Mary Tudor prisoner. Mary became aware of this and, with a handful of supporters, fled to East Anglia. From there she invoked the English people to observe natural justice and return her as the rightful heir to the throne. Her call was answered. Her right of inheritance took precedence over religious differences, and the people supported her cause. Within a matter of days all the conniving of Northumberland had come to nought. He acknowledged the fact and gave himself up, thereafter being incarcerated in the Tower where he and some of his closest associates were executed. Jane and her husband were initially sentenced to death but were spared as being mere pawns in the game. It was a treasonable event some time after, in which they took no active part, which caused Mary to reverse that decision. They were deemed guilty by association and executed.

Mary I

Mary was born in 1516. She took the throne in 1553. Unfortunately, Mary misinterpreted the initial enthusiasm demonstrated by the populace who supported her right to the throne. She imagined that they were celebrating the opportunity to return the country to Catholicism when in fact they, in typically English fashion, simply wanted justice to be done and be seen to be done, in the cause of succession.

One of her first acts was to reinstate the Roman Catholic prelates to their former eminence and to effect complete restoration of Catholic worship in England. Her decision to marry Philip II of Spain was met with dissent. Sir Thomas Wyatt raised an army against the forfeiture of Protestantism and the prospect of being merged with Spain, but the rebellion was crushed. It did revive the spectre of others being used to oppose Mary and provided the excuse to execute Lady Jane and her husband. Mary took the precaution to remove a perceived threat which might carry more potential and imprisoned Princess Elizabeth. Then began a campaign against heretics and about 300 perished at the stake including Thomas Cranmer, Ridley and Latimer, earning Mary the nickname 'Bloody Mary'. Sadly she found herself up to the neck in a whirlpool of events involving royal succession and religious reformation. Combining this with an unfortunate marriage to Philip II, whose cynical intention was merely to forge an alliance against France, spelt disaster. She would brook no interference in her plans and Philip's influence involved England in a war with France which ended in failure and the loss of Calais in 1558, after it had been held for 200 years. Mary died the same year, vilified for the number of people she consigned to be burned at the stake.

Elizabeth I

Elizabeth, daughter of Henry VIII and Anne Boleyn, was born in 1533, and ascended the throne in 1558.

She had overcome, or at least coped with, many difficult situations in her life before being named successor to the throne. Her father first divorced her mother and afterwards condemned her to be beheaded. After her brother Edward VI died she had to support her sister Mary, a committed Catholic, against the enthronement of Lady Jane Grey who was, like herself, a Protestant. This called for a delicate balancing act, because this was a time when religion played a crucial part in almost every aspect of life. As the next in line to the throne after her sister Mary, Elizabeth could conceivably be seen by Protestant conspirators as a vehicle by which they might overthrow Mary and again reverse the religious orientation of the country. Undoubtedly this made her vulnerable to all sorts of rumour and suspicions in a period when they were tantamount to evidence of treason. Indeed, in 1554, she was imprisoned in the Tower by Mary when dissidents were expressing their anger against Mary's repressive government.

Overcoming all these problems spoke volumes for Elizabeth's fortitude and diplomatic skill, which served her and England so well later in her reign. She had received a classical education under the tuition of William Grindal and Roger Ascham, which gave her the assurance to be able to apply both reason and logic to deal with the enormous responsibilities which she faced throughout her reign. Furthermore, she had a charismatic personality allied to an inherent feminine intuitiveness when dealing with people, which made her a formidable supporter, or opponent. She sometimes dispensed with logic, in favour of feminine guile, if it no longer suited her purpose. She selected her ministers and servants with judicious care. Mathew Parker, a moderate cleric, was chosen to be her adviser on all matters ecclesiastical. In 1535 he was chaplain to Anne Boleyn and then in 1537 to Henry VIII. When Mary became queen he went into hiding until 1558. He became Archbishop of Canterbury in 1559.

Parker was a meticulous man of enquiring mind and also liked to make sure that things were done properly and above board. This trait acquired for him the soubriquet 'Nosey' and he thereby had the dubious honour of being the original Nosey Parker. He died in 1575 but the nickname is still applied today to people who act in the same punctilious way.

A Parliament was called on 25 January 1559 and was dissolved on 8 May, having accomplished its objective. This was to prepare the nation for a return to the Reformed faith and a Parliament that was subject to the court.

Elizabeth's chief advisers pressed her to marry to secure future succession but she avowed that she would live and die a virgin. Among the suitors proposed for her were the Duc D'Alencon, Prince Erik of Sweden, the Archduke Charles of Austria and Philip of Spain. She showed consummate skill in temporising with these would-be husbands, usually to her political advantage.

History records that she was the best-loved sovereign ever to rule in England. It may have been because she had what Shakespeare called the 'common touch' that endeared her to the people, or that she simply possessed innate common sense in her day-to-day dealings with her subjects.

Religion still played a pivotal part but with some differences. Freed from the repressive rule of Mary Tudor, the Puritans began to demand that their dogmas should be predominant, which resulted in the Established Church constraining them in similar fashion to the previous regime. Elizabeth also had the problem of Mary Queen of Scots.

Mary's father was James V of Scotland, his queen and her mother, Mary of Lorraine, a princess in her own right.

She was brought up as a Catholic and at the age of 16 in 1558 was married to the Dauphin of France who was two years younger. On the death of his father in 1559 he inherited the throne as Francis II.

Mary's life seemed destined to be dogged by tragic influences. Her father died when she was only a few days old and her teenage husband Francis died within two years of becoming king of France. In August 1561 she returned to Scotland as a widow and rightful queen but once there she faced serious difficulties. First, as a committed Catholic she wanted to re-establish that religion in Scotland but found that the Scots were equally adamant that they preferred to remain Presbyterian. She came up against a formidable opponent in John Knox, the Scottish reformer. Over the next few years, after forfeiting her initial popularity, she became embroiled in all kinds of unpleasant and violent episodes, culminating in the Battle of Langside 1568. Afterwards she was forced to renounce her right to the throne of Scotland in favour of her infant son and was imprisoned. She escaped after about a year, came to England and begged to be given protection and an interview with Elizabeth. This was refused until she should be cleared of wrongdoing by her own former subjects; nevertheless, she was allowed to remain but in close confinement.

The whole situation was fraught with problems because if Elizabeth died Mary would be an obvious contender for the throne. The same would apply should Elizabeth be supplanted – therefore Mary was more than an embarrassment, she was a positive danger. As a potential rallying point for those disaffected Catholics who wanted a return to the Roman Church she represented an opportunity to achieve this. The Earls of Northumberland and Westmorland were the first to involve themselves in a conspiracy but like others detected and snuffed out. It did not end there however. Anthony Babington formed a plot against the life of the queen but it was discovered and he and his fellow conspirators were executed in September 1586.

Elizabeth herself had lived under the shadow of possible execution for some years during the violent reign of her sister Mary. The fact that she had provided safe haven, albeit with restrictions, for many years to her cousin, Mary Queen of Scots, was some indication of the empathy she felt. Although both Houses of Parliament called for the execution of Mary she still found it difficult to agree to sign the death warrant until another plot was uncovered in the December 1586. According to one learned source it was about this time that Mary wrote a long letter to Elizabeth in which she stated that she had 'a constant resolution to suffer death' as a martyr to her Catholic religion. Another month passed and tragically Mary's supporters were rumoured to be preparing a further attempt to overturn the sovereign. This finally gave the impetus to Elizabeth to sign the document which resulted in the execution of Mary on 1 February 1587.

During this period Protestants in many parts of Europe were being persecuted and Elizabeth gave assistance to the Huguenots in France and Protestants in the Netherlands. Henceforth in Europe, she was regarded as the Protestant standard-bearer. By this time, Philip of Spain was in a state of furious resentment against Elizabeth. She had spurned his offer of marriage, and was aiding the Netherlands to rid themselves of his tyrannical rule. Finally her maritime emissaries in the Caribbean had deprived him of much gold and influence by their piratical activities.

Apropos the foregoing there was another issue which began 40 years before Elizabeth was born. After the discoveries by Columbus in 1492, Pope Alexander VI, at the Treaty of Tordesillas in 1493, decided to divide the world between Portugal and Spain. He decreed that from a line drawn 370 leagues west of the Cape Verde Islands, all that lay west of the line was to be Spanish and all that lay east belonged to

Portugal. This is how it is generally described but presumably he was referring only to the newly-discovered territories. Whatever the interpretation of the treaty, the English refused to accept the Pope's jurisdiction and repeatedly entered those prohibited waters, actions which naturally brought them into conflict with Spanish fleets.

Inflamed by these provocations Philip devoted three years to assembling a mighty fleet with which, together with his powerful army, he intended to invade England. In 1587 Francis Drake delayed the invasion preparations by at least a year when he attacked and destroyed a large part of the fleet at anchor in the harbour of Cadiz. Nevertheless it did not sway the determination of the Spanish commanders, who in 1588 made good their threat. They loaded their ships with soldiers and set sail for England. This fleet consisted of 130 great war vessels larger and more powerful than any English ships of the time, 30 ships of war of a smaller size, more than 19,000 marines, almost 8,500 sailors, over 2,000 slaves and more than 2,600 cannon. All this was under the command of the Duke of Medina-Sidonia. The plan was to supplement them to an even greater extent by a land force from the Spanish-occupied Netherlands under the leadership of the Prince of Parma. They were in readiness to spearhead a land invasion on the south coast of England as the great Armada progressed through the English Channel.

The English fleet under the command of Lord Howard and his lieutenants Drake, Hawkins and Frobisher, intercepted the Spanish in the English Channel where they were attacked and dispersed. The story of how this victory was achieved is worthy of being read in greater detail as are the individual contributions of great sea captains and admirals who took part.

Elizabeth died on 23 March 1603, having earned for herself the title of 'Gloriana', worshipped by the people of England. Before she died she named James VI of Scotland as her successor. With this act she effectively created the union of England and Scotland, and he became James I of England, having sovereignty over both.

7

The British Empire

The English (and British) have been criticised, sometimes by their own countrymen, over the fact that they founded an empire which had a presence in almost every part of the world. One cannot claim that colonisation was maintained from motives of altruism, for at the outset it was primarily for trade. That it was received favourably, even encouraged by the local rulers, showed that it must have suited both parties.

It is probably fitting to examine India as an example of how changes came about. India then consisted of many individual states ruled by local princes and these leaders wielded ultimate powers within their own region. Permission to trade therefore was either given or withheld by them. From the outset the English were welcomed and after their early visits were allowed to set up a number of small commercial settlements, chief of which was at Surat.

The East India Company was formed in 1599, being granted a Charter by Queen Elizabeth I for the purpose of trade with the East Indies for a period of 15 years. The French, Portuguese and Dutch were also engaged in lucrative trade with many countries of the Far East and began to resent others intruding in what they regarded as their prerogative. The competition intensified with the Dutch and Portuguese sending out fully armed vessels which commenced harassing the English merchantmen until it became unprofitable for English investors to continue to underwrite the enterprise. An application was granted by the crown for some English ships to be armed and used as escort vessels. In 1613 an action at sea off Surat, to protect the eighth expedition, between the escort under Captain Best and a large Portuguese fleet, ended in complete defeat of the latter. It so impressed the Great Sultan of Murat that he granted the English (by treaty) full rights to trade in his dominions.

To avoid a repetition of violent confrontation, in 1619 a treaty was concluded with the Dutch guaranteeing harmonious trading relations between the two countries. Sadly this was broken by the Dutch in 1623 when they attacked and massacred the leading members of the English factory at Amboyna. Under the feeble reigns of the first two Stuart kings this deed remained unpunished but was addressed by Cromwell who took retaliatory action.

In 1639 the East India Company received a grant of land in the region of Madras from the Rajah of Bijnagar. By agreement a fort was erected. The first voyages were highly profitable and both parties must have been happy with the arrangement, otherwise the local rulers would have ejected the English at an early stage. Based on initial successes there was a substantial increase in the number of financial backers for the enterprise and by 1640 the English had secured territorial grants in Madras, plus the right to control all the factories in Bengal and on the Coromandel coast. Meanwhile their main council in India remained at Surat.

In 1660 new and enlarged powers were granted to the East India Company by Charles II which could be implemented by their factories and also allow them to appoint governors. The abuse of these powers was making the Company unpopular in India so the rights of the Company were withdrawn and a new one constituted by William III in 1698.

An important factor has to be noted at this juncture. In

1707 England and Scotland decided to sign the Act of Union thereby joining parliaments. From that time they would be known as Britain. What had started as an English enterprise would now become British, and Scots would henceforth be admitted to all parts of the world which had come into the fold of Westminster.

The French were continually strengthening their alliances with regional leaders. On the subcontinent it became evident that trade had become secondary to the acquisition of power. French influence was growing and they began exerting severe pressure against British settlements by enlisting military aid from their alliances with local princes. Finally, after a number of battles, by 1760 the French military presence in India was utterly defeated and it was this which led to India becoming a British colony.

Apart from the French, Dutch, Portuguese and English battling each other for dominance on the subcontinent many changes were being enacted among the leaders of the various groups either in India itself or on its borders. The reasons were not dissimilar except that they merely wanted control rather than trade. The Afghans and Mahrattas were invading the established Mogul Empire and were also fighting between themselves. Their attention began to turn against the British establishments, against which they formed alliances.

A memorable confrontation took place at Calcutta. The Nawab of Bengal, resentful of the encroachment by the British, gathered a large army and attacked and overcame the settlement on 21 June 1756. The survivors, 146 in all, were made prisoner and incarcerated in a small chamber. It was the garrison prison with only 18 square feet of space, originally intended to house a couple of miscreants. They were kept suffering terribly in stifling heat overnight. In the morning only 23 of them remained alive.

Robert Clive, 1725–1774

He obtained a post as a writer with the East India Company at Madras. After several years he resigned and entered military service in India. At the time, the prospects for the British in India were looking bleak. The French had made great gains in territory and also formed strong alliances. In 1751 Clive led a force composed of British and Indian troops against these forces and took the city of Arcot and, in taking the initiative against other important militarised areas, turned the tide of events by completely routing the enemy. He returned to Madras a hero but his health had suffered and he was obliged to return home for an extended period to recover.

Two years later he was back in India commanding the expedition to Bengal. The forces of Nabob Suraj-ud-Dowlah had attacked British factories and had taken Calcutta. They imprisoned and suffocated 120 of them in an incident named the Black Hole of Calcutta. Clive re-took Calcutta and later, in the Battle of Plassey, he defeated and deposed the former Nabob. There were many other victories and successes in store for him. Apart from his destruction of the French presence in India, he also repulsed the Dutch incursions.

He was not only renowned for military prowess but also for many improvements in the government of the country generally.

Having suffered much ill health, he died by his own hand in 1774.

Clive was despatched immediately from Madras. He retook the settlement and in 1757 routed the Nawab's forces at the Battle of Plassey. Further victories at Chandernagore and Masulipatam were added by Coote, who at Wanderwash in

1760 eliminated French power in India. Reflecting the political changes having taken place in what was now 'Great Britain' the regions then fell into the hands of the British. The earliest important figures of the time were Clive, Hastings and Wellesley, later to become famous as the Duke of Wellington.

It would seem that the transmutation from a trading partner to a colonising power came about somewhat bizarrely as a result of European powers squabbling over trading rights and concessions; using military means in the process and sometimes engaging the provincial ruler as an ally. If the victor proved to be the one who had no such alliance he not only gained, or retained, the trading rights but also wrested control of the province from the incumbent prince. Upon being defeated the local dignitaries were in the invidious position of a defeated enemy. If they wished to continue to enjoy their previous status and privileged lifestyle, they were forced to make the best accommodation possible. The difference being that their authority was now nominal and subservient to one which had no legitimate right to the territory, other than as a tenant. Thus, gradually, military rule supplanted what were formerly simply trading bases.

English (later British) involvement in the Far East, as we see, began as a commercial undertaking and eventually transformed into colonisation. It is a fact that many countries did undergo considerable change, culminating in British rule which still attracts strong opinions on whether or not it constituted exploitation. It is fair to claim that over the whole period in some respects much that was beneficial was left behind in the form of a commercial, political and social legacy which is driving the economies of many former colonies even today.

India was by far always the most important trading partner of England and eventually assumed even greater significance. The government at Westminster became concerned at the behaviour of the East India Company, upon which, over time, powers of government had devolved. These were removed from the company in 1858 and transferred to the British Crown. In 1877 Queen Victoria was proclaimed the Empress of India.

From then on, many enterprises were undertaken in an effort to enhance and modernise life and opportunities in the peninsular. Although many succeeded it would be folly to expect everyone to see it that way. India is a large country of immense diversity of people, languages, religion, culture, caste and origin. Nevertheless, at the turn of the twentieth century it was experiencing a major change, not least in its sense of unity as a single nation instead of a number of separate provinces. With this feeling came a growing desire to sever the cord binding the country to Britain and to take control of its own affairs. Certain factions were for outright instant independence achieved by revolutionary methods, whereas the more cerebral resolved to take a diplomatic path. It was the arrival of a great man of peace called Mahatma Gandhi that finally solved the problem. He had been to university in London and later trained as a barrister. His use of legal knowledge to present the case was invaluable. Allied to these attributes he campaigned tirelessly by means of non-cooperation. His aspirations were rewarded soon after the Second World War when, after great deliberation between heads of government, it was decided when and how independence would be achieved. Although his vision was to have an India completely united in every sense, this task was beyond even him.

The insuperable obstacle was that of religion. In 1947 when the governments of Great Britain and India reached agreement on independence the only question to be answered was how could it be achieved equably and peacefully. The leaders of all parties concerned convened to decide. The Muslim faith and some other religions in India, particularly Hinduism, were so distinct from one another that it was decided that the only practical solution was to partition the country to enable each to determine its own future. Pressures mounted from either side for a very early date to be set. Concerns were raised that it might be too precipitate but under the demands it was conceded. The fears proved to be well founded because the process of hundreds of thousands of families uprooting themselves from homes in which they and their forebears had lived for generations proved to be more inflammatory than had been envisaged. People on both sides of what had become a border separating two different countries were in a state of confusion physically and emotionally. Unfortunately this became an explosive mixture resulting in considerable animosity and bloodshed. The saddest epitaph of all is that Gandhi, who did so much for all the people of India, whatever their faith, was assassinated by one of his own people.

The Achievements of the British Raj

By the early part of the twentieth century the following advances were taking, or had already taken, place.

Rather than the British occupying most administrative positions, the Indian people themselves were entering every aspect of life, both administratively and in government, forming the essential and tangible requirements of infrastructure essential to the efficient running of a modern country. So comprehensive was this change that thoughts were surfacing which questioned the concept of remaining as a colony. India was no longer at war with itself so why should it need help or direction from another country?

The British had been instrumental in putting in place all of the features which made such an aspiration possible. Whatever the rights and wrongs which may be argued, it is hard to think of any other colonising nation that has left so all-embracing a legacy in place as that of India.

Irrigation Canals and the Telegraph

Extensive irrigation programmes amounting to roughly 40,000,000 acres were put in place supplying the wherewithal to encourage or extend cultivation programmes, converting barren areas into fertile farmland. Canals were constructed to enable the transport of produce. Existing canals were extended. By the beginning of the twentieth century a countrywide telegraph system had been installed.

Railways

Prior to the introduction of railways, India's means of transportation and trade was the Rivers Ganges and Indus. The railways built by the British comprehensively connected India's provinces for both trade and passenger traffic, covering an estimated 50,000 miles in all by 1940. The staff to run and maintain the system at all levels were recruited and trained by the British.

Horticulture

Non-indigenous plants from other parts of the Empire or countries with whom England traded, notably tea (about a million acres), rubber (about 250,000 acres) and coffee (about 200,000 acres) were introduced and planted. This brought employment to thousands of workers and more prosperity to the country generally. In common with other former colonies the benefits of this programme are evident today and underpin their economies. The plants themselves were collected during various voyages, largely by the botanists of Kew Gardens in London where they were propagated into healthy plants before being transported to various countries with climatic conditions conducive to successful cultivation. One plant worth mentioning is the Chinchona (or Cinchona) tree, the bark of which was discovered to have curative medicinal properties to reduce fevers and was effective in countering the effects of malaria. The plant originates from the eastern side of the Andes, Peru, Bolivia, Ecuador and Colombia in South America. It takes its name from the Countess of Chinchon, a lady who was cured of fever in 1638 by medicine derived from the bark. Like the cork tree, the bark, if removed carefully, is capable of naturally self-renewing.

Exponents of what can be best described as 'botanical economics' used their knowledge and expertise to identify plants which would grow successfully and profitably in other parts of the world. As the British Empire had colonies scattered all over the globe there were plenty of opportunities for them to prove their theories. The results had a profound effect on the future wealth and well-being of many regions. Their first objective was to estimate the value, in economic terms, of practicable transplantation of a particular species of plant. Particular attention was paid to the growing conditions necessary for the plants to flourish in the new location. English botanists travelled all over the world collecting the seeds of such plants which they sent to Kew for germination and cultivation. Once satisfactory results had been obtained the plants were packed and dispatched to the various countries selected for plantations to be established. The far-sightedness of their work can be seen in the number of former British colonies whose economies, even today, are still benefiting from the programme. Listed below are some of those most prominent in developing the scheme.

Botanical Economists of the Empire

Exponents of what can be best described as Botanical Economics used their knowledge and expertise to identify plants which would grow successfully and profitably in other parts of the world. As the British Empire had colonies scattered all over the globe, there were plenty of opportunities for them to prove their theories. The results had a profound effect on the future wealth and well-being of many regions. Their first objective was to estimate the value, in economic terms, of practicable transplantation of a particular species of plant. Particular attention was paid to the growing conditions necessary for the plants to flourish in the new location. English botanists travelled all over the world collecting seeds of suitable plants which they sent to Kew for germination and cultivation. Once satisfactory results had been obtained, the plants were packed and despatched to the various countries selected for plantations to be established. The far-sightedness of their work can be seen in the number of former British colonies whose economies, even today, are still benefitting from the programme. Listed below are some of those most prominent in developing the scheme.

Joseph Banks, 1743–1820

A botanist who managed Kew Gardens from 1772 to 1819. In the course of his search for plants he sailed to many parts of the world with Captain Cook. He sent botanists to different parts of the world on a similar quest for new species of potentially economic benefit. His influence may be judged by the fact that at the end of his career he left Kew with a collection of plants numbered in thousands.

William Jackson Hooker, 1785–1865

Noted botanist and director of Kew. From 1821 to 1841 he was Professor of Botany at Glasgow University following which he was appointed director of Kew Gardens. He wrote extensively on botanical subjects.

Joseph Dalton Hooker, 1809–1880

Son of the above. Studied medicine at the University of Glasgow but later became interested in botany. He accompanied Sir James Ross on an Antarctic expedition in the Erebus in 1839, afterwards publishing an account of the flora of the area. In 1848 he led a botanical expedition to Northern India. Appointed an assistant director at Kew in 1855, he succeeded his father as director in 1858, a post he held until he retired in 1885. He was a close friend of Charles Darwin and it was through his and Sir Charles Lyell's entreaties that Darwin was persuaded to publish his first statement of the theory of natural selection.

Clement R. Markham, 1830–1916

One of the leading figures in reshaping the economies of the British colonies in the Far East by the introduction of plants which could become 'cash crops'. The principal ones were tea, rubber and tobacco. Others such as the Chinchona (see above) he transported from its native habitat of South America. In cooperation with Hooker Jnr he was largely responsible for establishing the rubber industry in South Asia.

Nick H. Ridley, 1855–1956

Botanist and director of the Singapore Botanical Gardens. Another whose interests went beyond the normal boundaries of a botanist, he too was interested in the economics of plant movement. He was very much influenced by the work of Joseph Hooker. He was also responsible for establishing the rubber industry on the Malay peninsula.

George H.K. Thwaites, 1840–1910

Botanist and director of Sri Lankan Peradeniya Botanical Gardens. During the 1870s he introduced tea and rubber plantations to the country. These crops were vital to the restoration of the economy which had lost its main source of income when the coffee disease of 'rust infestation' wiped out the entire crop.

Government

A secular form of government was instituted, in accordance with various parliamentary statutes incorporated in the Government of India Acts, enacted during the early part of the twentieth century. Legislature consisted of two houses, one the Council of State, the other an elected legislative assembly which was created in 1921.

Administration

An apolitical Civil Service was created to administer the affairs of state. This Civil Service was originally recruited from British applicants. Gradually and for a long time before independence it changed to being run predominantly by the Indian people themselves. To obtain such a post entailed a considerable amount of study and educational ability. Any British applicant was, in addition to the normal requirements, obliged to be fluent in at least one Indian language, whereas those from India were obliged to be able to speak English.

Law

An independent judiciary was founded and trained to apply the laws of the land impartially. A police force was organised in such a way as to be an independent body and not to enforce the law in the manner of a police state. As in Britain, they themselves were not above the law and worked closely in harmony with both the government and judiciary. In a country with a complicated caste system this was no mean achievement.

Education

Schools and universities were founded and many important subjects including the English language taught to a high level. Students leaving these establishments usually entered the various arms of the Indian governmental structure – i.e. the police service, Civil Service, railways, teaching, government, the judiciary or other essential services. The use of English has had a positive effect in all of these groups because in a large country with approximately 220 different languages it simplifies communication, even today. It also eliminates the possibility of one regional language becoming dominant and allows all to be eligible to apply for any position, provided they have the qualifications.

Independence

Little wonder that when the time came in 1947 for the demand for independence to be recognised these various and solidly based institutions paved the way for a relatively smooth transition of power and happily ensured that India remained not only one of our most valued allies but one of the best democratically governed countries in the world.

It might be worth considering that barely a hundred years

before the arrival of the English, the country had been invaded by the Moguls who divided much of it into tribal areas. Their form of control was, in essence, probably no more autocratic than that which initially developed under the British, the difference being that under British rule the regions were brought together, thereby creating a unified country rather than a number of fragmented states. That this was achieved is not claimed to be part of a master plan by the British for the benefit of India, but more probably occurred to simplify central control. Nevertheless, the possibilities are small that so many differing cultures, owing allegiance to so many regional autocrats, would ever have progressed towards the democratic form of government which finally evolved, consciously or unconsciously, under British rule.

There is no gainsaying the fact that the British made many mistakes during their long stay on the subcontinent, but they were also responsible for changes which have had lasting benefit. Whatever criticisms are made of the years of British rule, by the time of the outbreak of the Great War of 1914–1918 relations between Britain and the subcontinent were sufficiently cordial for them to generously support Britain with troops and finance. The cooperation continued during the Second World War with Indian troops serving alongside the British in Europe, and again when India was threatened by the Japanese army invading through South-east Asia into Burma. It has not ended there: the Gurkha regiment still serves with the British army and has served with great distinction wherever it has been deployed.

After many nations, which were formerly part of the British Empire, became independent, the Empire was superseded by an organisation called 'The Commonwealth of Nations'. It was considered that there were many ties binding Britain and its former colonies together, not least aid and trade, which would be furthered by cooperative action among equal members.

It should not be forgotten that some requested to remain as colonies, and were not refused. The establishment of the Commonwealth has been for the most part a successful project. It has demonstrated that, in the long term, British rule, although far from perfect, had not been as bad as some critics would have us believe. It was an achievement not mirrored by other colonial powers. In fact, some African countries, not previously part of the British Empire, actually applied to be accepted for Commonwealth membership because their previous colonial masters had simply walked away, leaving them rudderless. Incidentally, Britain, and principally England, now has the largest population of people of Indian origin of any country outside India itself.

Some countries, particularly in Africa, had become reasonably self-sufficient, commanding a healthy place in world markets for their products, especially those introduced by the British such as coffee and tea. Products like these could have formed the basis for continued economic development but unfortunately they fell victim to the clamour of agitators who, in pursuit of ultimate personal power, inflamed their countrymen in the demand for independence before a sustainable infrastructure for modern government had been established. Sadly these would-be leaders were or are despots and have misled their people and killed millions while subjecting them to a tyranny far worse than anything experienced under the rule of the British Empire.

Sports and games

Of all the sports and games which enthral millions of sports enthusiasts around the world, most originated in England. In addition, all games which were played on grass were revolutionised by the invention of the lawnmower by Englishman Edwin Budding in the early 1800s. First designed for creating a more decoratively cut lawn, their potential for other applications soon became evident. Football and hockey pitches, tennis courts, bowling greens etc. all started to use them to improve the playing surface.

Association Football (Soccer)

Although people have played with round objects made from all kinds of materials for hundreds and maybe thousands of years, they bore little resemblance to a sporting activity. In fact many descended into an excuse for a legalised fight. Football was played in fourteenth century England and is mentioned by Chaucer. It was forbidden during the reign of Edward I because it was deemed detrimental to the practice of archery. It was in nineteenth century England when it was decided that here was a pastime in which organised teams, acting in accordance with established rules, could be developed into a true sport. Played in the right spirit it is regarded by most as the development of 'the pure game'.

The Football Association was formed in 1863. Leagues were formed and additional competitions held at which silver cups were awarded. The game was received enthusiastically by other countries and is now administered by a European body, FIFA. Without question it is the most popular game ever devised and is now played and enjoyed by practically every nation on earth. To most it has become their national game.

Nowadays, apart from the World Cup there are national, continental and sub-continental competitions. These games often take place between nations who previously had little in common other than a border and an abundance of hostility. It is also an Olympic sport.

Cricket

Devised by the English at the turn of the eighteenth century cricket is now played in many countries, principally but not all, previously part of the British Empire and now voluntary members of the Commonwealth. In some countries it is the national game and has taken the skill factor to exceptional levels.

Rugby Union

Another version of football, rugby is a major sport which takes the spirit of sportsmanship to the highest level and is continuing to spread throughout the world. It was first played at Rugby School in about 1823, at first mainly by school teams who produced their own rule book to which competing teams adhered. As the game spread a governing body for the sport in general came into being in 1871, issuing rules under which it was agreed it would be governed.

Rugby League

An almost identical form of the game is known as rugby league and is concentrated in the north of England in a few counties. The only differences are that it has always been a semi-professional or professional game and conforms to a different set of rules.

Hockey

Started in south London in the middle of the nineteenth century, this is a demanding game requiring a high level of fitness and dexterity, overseen by the Hockey Association. It has gained the status of an Olympic sport.

Tennis

The modern game of tennis was first practised in the Midlands of England in the middle of the nineteenth century. Rules for the game were drawn up in London in 1875. Like the others it is now a truly global game. Wimbledon is still the tournament the greats of the sport all aspire to win.

Badminton

This game originated at the estate of the Duke of Beaufort in the nineteenth century when it was called 'shuttle-cock' but was later renamed after the duke's home.

Swimming

The English were the first to develop swimming as a competitive sport, to build swimming pools of set lengths dedicated to that purpose, and have defined distances for competition. Other countries followed suit and it has now become a major part of the Olympic games.

Boxing

A form of fist fighting was commonplace even in ancient Roman times. In those days they used to wrap the fists with metal straps in which spikes were fitted which were intended to either maim or kill the opponent. Bare-knuckle fighting was common in England in the eighteenth century. The fights were illegal and were set up in out of the way country spots in secrecy, being attended by the young bucks of the period. Naturally there was a great deal of gambling on the outcome of a contest. There were no concessions regarding size and weight and a contest was decided when one contestant could no longer 'come up to the mark'. Without proper supervision injuries could be severe, one fighter nicknamed 'Hen' Pearce continuing to fight for years despite losing an eye in a contest. Others like Tom Sayers became national heroes. Others opened gymnasiums to teach the art of self-defence and it was one of these who saw the folly in the lack of proper control over what was becoming a regularly attended activity.

His name was Jack Broughton and in England in 1743 he put forward a set of rules under which boxing bouts would take place. He also introduced a type of boxing glove. Under his guidance boxing went from being an activity of largely unorganised and brutal fighting and an excuse for a wager, to something which was elevated to the status of becoming a regulated sport. This eventually led to the development of amateur boxing and both amateur and professional codes. The new regulations ensured that boxers were segregated into different weights with additional safeguards for the matching of contestants in skill and experience. Amateur boxing is a major Olympic sport.

Table Tennis

Formerly known as ping-pong, table tennis began in England during the early part of the twentieth century and gained popularity so quickly that within a matter of a few years the world championships were held in London. It is estimated that more than 7 million people enjoy the game in China alone.

Squash

Squash was played by the students at Harrow school in the nineteenth century and became rapidly popular. The English National Association was formed in early 1920s and today well over 50 countries have organised associations to supervise the game. It is also an Olympic sport.

Darts

Darts started as a game played in pubs in nineteenth-century England but since the Second World War its popularity has soared and it now holds world championships.

Snooker

Snooker attracts professional competitors from many countries. Tournaments are frequently held in countries in various parts of the world. This game, if no more skilful than its progenitor billiards, is more complicated and more interesting for the spectator. It was originally devised by British troops serving in India.

Horse racing (the sport of kings)

To race a horse was common practice in England in the middle ages as a sales-aid to bump-up the value of an animal during horse trading. In this respect it was probably no different from what was practised by people of other countries. Racing for money, however, has been recorded in England as early as the twelfth century.

The English seem to have an inclination to turn almost every activity into an organised sport to be enjoyed by participants and spectators alike, embodying rules which must be adhered to, thus allowing skill and endeavour to be the deciding factors and ensuring fair competition. Horse racing is no exception. Hence the governing body, known as the Jockey Club, was founded in 1750 to administer the sport.

The conclusions it reached were that fair and open competition could best be attained by matching animals of similar physical strain or type, but how? There existed dozens of types of horse in the world, all bred for differing purposes. The only solution was to select horses with the preferred attributes and begin a selective breeding programme. As a horse grows to maturity in a relatively short span of time, this was considered workable. Among the native types one was chosen and the search began to decide which types, from other parts of the world, could be bred with it to produce the ideal animal for the purpose of racing.

The final selection resulted in the importation of a small number of stallions of Arab, Turkish and Berber origin. They were animals, prized highly not merely for their physical beauty but also for their agility, speed and spirit. These were allied to our native animal possessing strength and endurance. The resultant strain of horse became the thoroughbred race-horse of today. Now, not only is the sport of racing, under the same rules, enjoyed in many countries throughout the world but it has become almost an industry in its own right.

Some of the great classic races of the world are still the Derby, the Grand National, the St Leger and the Oaks. Every year expert racehorse breeders from Ireland, France, America and Australia are welcomed to our shores to contest these prestigious events just as our animals travel to theirs.

8

English Scientists

In common with their counterparts in other parts of the world, English scientists were usually regarded with a certain amount of suspicion and mistrust. The earlier the age in which experiment occurred, the more science came into conflict with superstition and many scientists were accused of sorcery. Listed below are a few, selected from the aristocracy of creative thought, to whom we should be grateful for persevering with their endeavours.

Roger Bacon, 1214–1294

Bacon was an English monk who is considered to be the founder of experimental science and was one of the most profound and original thinkers of his time. He first entered the University of Oxford, and went afterwards to that of Paris, where, after distinguishing himself as a scholar, he was awarded the degree of Doctor of Theology.

He returned to England and to the order of the Franciscans but incurred the displeasure of the ecclesiastical authorities for continuing with his scientific experiments and was sent back to Paris, where he was kept in close confinement for ten years without books, writing materials or instruments.

He conducted experiments in optics, chemistry, explosives,

engines and even mechanical flight (this being some 150 years before Leonardo da Vinci). He deduced results which appeared so extraordinary, even to people of high intelligence, that they were considered to be the works of magic; in order to achieve them, people believed he must be in league with Satan.

Some sources attribute the invention of gunpowder to him, possibly due to the fact that he wrote about it in 1242. It is thought, however, that he perceived it as an explosive, not a propellant.

He was also knowledgeable in geography and astronomy, as evidenced by his discovery of errors in the calendar, their causes, and his proposals for correcting them which were later considered to be very nearly exact. His persistence in pursuing his experiments once again invoked a charge against him of being in league with Satan and resulted in his suffering a further ten years of imprisonment. To a man of such towering intellect the denial of the ability to continue his work during the many years of incarceration must have exerted great mental strain on him. Who knows what his discoveries and experiments might have unearthed had he lived in a more enlightened time.

Christopher Wren, 1631–1723

Educated at Oxford, Wren later became Professor of Astronomy at that university. Several years later, he was appointed by the government of Charles II to restore St Paul's Cathedral.

The cathedral was situated on Ludgate hill which from early times had been the site of a church. The first was caused to be built by King Ethelbert in 610 and was burned to the ground in 1087. Old St Paul's was then built but suffered damage by fire twice in 1137 and 1561. It was also struck by lightning in 1444. When it was engulfed by the

Great Fire of London 1666 it became obvious that it had to be demolished.

The ruins remained undisturbed for at least seven years before a government decision was reached and Wren was charged with the task of designing and building a replacement. The whole project was overseen by Wren alone and took 35 years in all to complete.

Wren also designed and built 52 other churches in London, designed the modern part of the Palace of Hampton Court, the hospitals of Chelsea and Woolwich and the library of Trinity College Cambridge.

Robert Hooke, 1635–1703

A man of eclectic thought and ingenuity. His work, which examined the effects of stresses and strains on all manner of materials, enabled him to state and define the laws governing elasticity in his papers, published in 1678. The observance of these laws is present in all branches of applied mechanics – Hooke's Law states that 'in elastic bodies stress is proportional to strain'.

As a product of his genius he used his mechanical studies and inventiveness to devise the Universal Joint. It is a device designed to transmit a continual rotational motive force between two shafts which are not exactly parallel. It is still used extensively in many industrial applications, not least motor car manufacturing, which would indicate that it was at least a couple of hundred years before its time.

In 1664 he became the Professor of Mechanics to the Royal Society. He was also responsible for the rebuilding of London after the Great Fire of 1666.

Isaac Newton, 1642–1727

Born at Woolsthorpe, Lincolnshire, Newton is possibly the greatest genius of all time. He specified the laws of motion and gravitation. His work in pure mathematics, optics and the nature and origin of the spectra, together with the discoveries of the principle of calculus remain as evidence of his originality. His activities in the field of optics resulted in the invention of the reflecting telescope. He also explained the forces governing planetary behaviour in a great work on dynamics and astronomy, *Philosophiae Naturalis Principia Mathematica*, composed in 1686 and 1687.

It is as the discoverer of what he described as the 'Doctrine of Fluxions', now known as calculus, that he is regarded as having made the deepest impact on the history of mathematics.

Edmund Halley, 1656–1742

Halley correlated the comets with the solar system and calculated that 'Halley's comet' could be predicted to return into the earth's atmosphere at given frequencies. In 1682 he predicted correctly that the comet would return in 1789. He spent two years (1676–1678) on the island of St Helena from where he catalogued the stars of the southern hemisphere and arranged them into constellations.

John Hadley, 1682–1744

Hadley invented the quadrant which was used for calculating the altitude of heavenly bodies. These calculations were then used in navigation, surveying, gunnery and to further the science of astronomy. He subsequently invented the sextant and also made improvements to the reflecting telescope which had been invented earlier by Isaac Newton. (Newton also claimed part of the credit for the quadrant because of earlier information on the subject which he had supplied to Hadley).

John Harrison, 1693–1776

Harrison invented the chronometer and in so doing revolutionised the art of marine navigation, providing mariners with accurate information as to their true position at sea under all conditions. At the time there were astronomers of note who could calculate latitude but none could work out the longitude of a ship at sea. In a quest to overcome this deficiency, which was costing so many lives and ships, the merchant underwriters of the voyages and those who sailed the vessels actively urged the government to seek a scientific solution.

Their anxieties were given support from the navy who were also losing men and warships as a result of disasters caused by inaccurate navigation. An Act of Parliament was passed in 1714 offering rewards of £10,000, £15,000 or £20,000 to anyone who could provide a method of ascertaining longitude within 60, 40 or 30 miles.

John Harrison was the son of a carpenter and assisted his father in the business. He was self-educated but very inventive. His father occasionally mended clocks for other people and John obviously gleaned some knowledge of the construction of timepieces during the course of assisting him.

Harrison decided to manufacture a timepiece which could overcome the problems of changing temperatures or movement of a ship and give an accurate time. After many years of painstaking effort he was finally awarded the prize of the highest amount. His chronometer was proved to be near perfect.

During the process he mastered the principle of the different expandability of metals. Another of his inventions was a fusee (conical pulley or wheel on which the chain is wound and which equalises the power of the mainspring); this enabled a watch to be wound without interrupting its movements.

Henry Cavendish, 1731–1810

Cavendish was a physicist and chemist of the highest calibre. He is said to have anticipated Faraday, Black and Coulomb in some of his findings. He discovered the peculiar properties of hydrogen and the composition of water. He also wrote extensively on electricity.

The 'Cavendish Experiment' was an important experiment first carried out by Cavendish for the purpose of ascertaining the density of the earth.

Joseph Priestley, 1733–1804

Priestley was a man possessing an original intellect and who had many interests, including education, theology, politics, philosophy and science. His views on some of these subjects were unorthodox, bringing him into conflict with other bodies of opinion almost all the time. He was an atheist and declared Socinian which brought him much unpopularity. He also supported the French Revolution and this on one occasion in 1791 caused a hostile rabble to set fire to his house. His chief claim to fame, however, was his outstanding contribution to science. He was recognised by the Royal Society in 1766 and elected to its fellowship principally on the basis of his research into electricity.

The History and Present State of Electricity was published in 1767, and stated his findings as well as anticipating the results of later and more well-publicised researchers. The book includes the law of the inverse square in electrostatics and the oscillatory nature of the discharge of the Leyden jar. He then turned his attention to chemistry. This came about because of the processes carried out in a brewery which was located near his house and which he found interesting.

In 1774, by applying heat to mercuric oxide, he obtained oxygen and also discovered the eight gases now known as nitrogen, hydrochloric acid, nitrous oxide, ammonia, carbonic oxide, sulphur dioxide, nitric oxide and silicon tetrafluouride. He was the first to use the method of collecting gases in a pneumatic trough over mercury.

Priestley discovered the gas which was later called oxygen but named it dephlogisticated air. Lavoisier, a scientist in France, studied the techniques by which Priestley had achieved his breakthrough and opined that it was identical to air and gave it the name oxygen (from Greek: oxys, acid and root gen). His supposition was that it existed as the active constituent of all acids. The name oxygen was accepted by the scientific world and its function in combustion, also proved by Lavoisier, was acknowledged to be accurate. It would seem that although Priestley isolated the gas, his refusal to accept that his belief in its behaviour was mistaken cost him the reputation of the Father of Modern Chemistry.

Sir Humphrey Davy, 1778–1829

Davy invented the safety lamp for miners, known as the 'Davy lamp'. He also discovered sodium, potassium, calcium and chloride and the properties of 'laughing gas', later used in minor operations and dentistry. He was the first to employ electric current in chemical decomposition and discovered that nitrous oxide was safely respirable.

Michael Faraday, 1791–1867

One of the greatest English chemists and physicists, Faraday was born into humble circumstances at Newington Butts, London.

Early in life he was able to gain an apprenticeship with a bookbinder but in his spare time he occupied himself with electrical and other scientific experiments. He came to the notice of Sir Humphry Davy who appointed him as his assistant.

Faraday's researches in electrolysis laid the foundations of electro-chemistry and were followed by many important discoveries in electro-dynamics (including the laws which are the basis of modern electrical power) and in various departments of pure and applied chemistry, particularly the liquefaction of gases. The manufacture of glass also occupied his interest and he developed new types of optical glass. Indeed, there were few areas to escape his enquiring mind as evidenced by his discoveries regarding metallic alloys and the vaporisation of mercury. His invention of the generator led to the development of the dynamo.

Charles Babbage, 1791–1871

Generally regarded as the 'father of the computer', Babbage graduated from Cambridge University in 1814 and occupied the Lucasian Chair of Mathematics at that university for 11 years.

As early as 1812 he contemplated the possibilities of building a machine capable of calculating numerical tables. He named it 'The Difference Engine'.

In 1823 after receiving a grant from the government for that purpose, he began to build such a machine. He conceived the idea that by a system of cogs interconnected with columns of numbers and operated by a crank handle, the required calculations would automatically be produced.

During a period of about eight years of experiments and the expenditure of £17,000 (it is claimed that about a third of this sum was his contribution and the rest came from the government) he finally abandoned the project in favour of another and much more complex machine which he called his 'Analytical Engine'. This was operated with punched cards like the Jacquard loom. Unfortunately, having once more run out of money he did not quite complete the machine. It was, however, completed by a team at the Science Museum, London, where it now resides.

Charles Wheatstone, 1802–1875

Before he was 18 Wheatstone had set up in business in London as a maker of musical instruments. In 1823 he attracted the interest of the scientific world by publishing a paper entitled 'New Experiments of Sound'. This was followed by a series of papers describing a number of his own inventions, which were regarded highly for their ingenious design and excellence of mechanical construction. He invented the electric clock, the concertina and the stereoscope.

In 1834 Wheatstone was appointed Professor of Experimental Philosophy at King's College, London, where in 1836 he demonstrated some of his experiments showing the velocity of electricity and how it could be applied to the use of the electric telegraph. In 1837 together with William Cooke he took out a patent for the electric telegraph.

Joseph W. Swan, 1828–1914

Swan invented the incandescent electric lamp bulb, but did not patent it until a patent dispute a few years later. While he was engaged in researching the way to produce the filament for the lamp he discovered a method of producing artificial fibre.

He first won fame as an inventor in photography for his discovery of the autotype process and of making rapid dry plates. Other inventions included an electric safety lamp for miners, bromide paper for photography, improvements in photo-mechanical printing and electro-metallurgy.

William Crookes, 1832–1919

A physicist and chemist, Crookes carried out important research in connection with molecular physics, radiant matter and high vacua. One of his inventions was the radiometer, an instrument which has been employed to investigate the distribution of heat in the solar spectrum.

His findings revived work on cathode rays and the glass tubes he used to produce his results were henceforth named Crookes tubes. It should be remembered that it was the cathode tube, which excited such interest in the latter part of the nineteenth century, which became the solution in the 1930s to achieving a clearer television picture capable of professional broadcasting.

John A.R. Newlands, 1837-1898

Newlands catalogued the atomic structure of chemical elements. He published his findings, which he called the 'Law of Octaves' in 1884. A later work, *On the Discovery of the Periodic Law*, is in the main fully accepted.

Ernest Rutherford, 1871–1937

Born in New Zealand of English emigrant parents, although Rutherford is a national hero in the land of his birth, in view of the closeness of his relationship to England he could not be left out.

A physicist, in 1894 he won a science scholarship with which he proceeded to Cambridge, entering Trinity College, where he began on work in the Cavendish laboratory. In 1898 he went to McGill University, Canada, as Professor of Physics, where he began a study of radioactivity which he continued after returning to work in Manchester.

In 1919 he discovered a reaction between a nitrogen nucleus and an alpha particle. He was a leading world figure in atomic science and won the Nobel Prize for chemistry 1908.

Ambrose J. Fleming, 1881–1955

Fleming was the inventor of the thermionic valve, an important step in the progress of wireless telegraphy and also provided the link needed to develop wireless telephony.

Edward Appleton, 1892–1965

Appleton discovered the 'Appleton layer', a layer of the ionosphere 60 miles above the earth which reflects radio waves back to the surface. The same principle could be used to locate any solid object and led scientists to conduct further investigations which resulted in the development of radar and the considerable improvement of long-distance radio.

Bernard Lovell, 1913–

Lovell who founded the Jodrell Bank Experimental Station, where in 1957 he built the world's largest radio telescope. It was invaluable for accurately pinpointing the positions of earth satellites and space probes plus engaging in radio transmissions, especially when the first space missions were taking place.

Tim Berners-Lee, 1955–

The inventor of the World Wide Web which transformed the internet from an ordinary electronic means of communication into a previously unimaginable source of global information.

9

Inventors and Engineers

Dud Dudley, 1599–1684

One of the most urgent requirements during the sixteenth and seventeenth centuries was the manufacture of iron, much of which was for armaments.

The traditional method of smelting basic iron ore was to produce the necessary heat by first burning wood to produce charcoal. This conversion was necessary because charcoal when used in a furnace is capable of being raised to very high temperatures and much greater heat than raw wood itself.

This wasteful process was destroying the forests to an alarming degree, to the concern of the government of the time. Dudley experimented with the use of coke, a derivative of bituminous coal, and was so successful that he was granted a patent in 1621.

Marquis of Worcester, 1601–1667

Inventor of an early steam pump around 1645 which could raise water 40 feet, inspiring many who followed to improve on this idea. He was another visionary who foresaw many possible innovations and wrote a book entitled *A Century of*

Inventions, predicting aircraft, telegraphy and other developments. The most remarkable part of this man's life is that he wrote his book during the Civil War while he was imprisoned in the Tower of London by Cromwell for being a Royalist spy.

Thomas Savery, 1650–1715

Invented and patented in 1698 the first practical steam pump with hand-operated valves which used condensed steam to create suction to raise water from mines.

Thomas Newcomen, 1663–1729

In 1705 Newcomen developed a more efficient steam engine using a piston to compress the steam produced. However, the machine, although practical, was still inefficient but he had provided the basic design upon which improvements would later be made.

Abraham Darby, 1675–1717

In 1708 Darby patented a method of smelting iron by using coke, and some people credit him with being the first to explore the method. The fact of the matter appears to be that his patent differed from Dudley Dud's system only in that it enabled thinner metal to be produced, thereby rendering the end products and castings to be of a finer quality. His grandson followed in his tradition of iron smelting and casting and in 1779 cast and built the famous Ironbridge over the River Severn, the first cast iron bridge ever constructed. It is now a national monument.

Jethro Tull, 1694–1741

Tull was the first to introduce mechanisation to the English farm and thus eventually to world farming. He designed and produced a combined seed drilling, ploughing and cultivating machine which was the forerunner of all modern farm equipment.

Thomas Bolsover, 1706–1788

Bolsover discovered (by accident) the method of fusing silver onto copper. He was trying apparently to repair a silver knife and to hold it clamped in the vice he used a copper coin. During the process he overheated the metals and noticed that they had fused. Realising the possibilities he went on to experiment by using a similar process to apply a thin coating of silver to various copper articles. The method was successful and the resulting product became known as 'Sheffield plate' and developed into an industry in itself. It was the precursor of the later method of electroplating. Another of his inventions was the technique of making high carbon saw-blade steel by rolling it into sheet of the required thickness.

James Brindley, 1716–1772

Brindley was a brilliant engineer who was engaged by the Duke of Bridgewater to build a navigable canal to link his estate at Worsley with the towns of Manchester and Liverpool, for the purpose of transportation of coal and other materials by barge. By means of aqueducts over rivers and valleys he accomplished this between the years 1761 and 1765. The Bridgewater Canal has a length of 38 miles and is one of the earliest and most celebrated, although when it was first proposed it was the subject of ridicule by those who were unable to see the potential of this mode of transport.

The canal managed to become even more famous during the construction of the Manchester Ship Canal, when it became necessary to convert the Barton aqueduct, which crossed the Manchester Ship Canal at a point between Eccles and Trafford Park, from a standard aqueduct into one which swivelled on a central axis. This was positioned so that when it turned 90 degrees there was sufficient space in the centre of the Ship Canal for the passage of the seagoing liners on their way into docks which were located almost in the centre of Manchester. It should be noted that when the swivelling aqueduct was so positioned it was locked off at either end so that it still contained a section of canal. This meant that one canal was operating over the top of another.

Another great work undertaken by Brindley was the Grand Trunk Canal uniting the Trent and Mersey.

John Roebuck, 1718–1794

Roebuck was a chemist, physician and inventor who founded the Carron ironworks in Scotland in 1749 using the smelting method devised by Dud Dudley. He also invented a method of mass-producing sulphuric acid in lead chambers and opened a factory at Prestonpans near Edinburgh for the production of sulphuric acid. This was a breakthrough for the bleaching industry for whom the process of bleaching cloth was laborious and usually unpleasant.

John Roebuck was a member of the 'Lunar Society', a group of English inventors and entrepreneurs who met frequently to pool their ideas for the betterment of industry. In addition to his other enterprises he was also sinking a deep shaft for coal at Boroughstoness in Scotland. The pump he was using was by Newcomen and was not efficient enough for the deep mining techniques now being developed. He was actively seeking someone to produce an improved model which would give that extra power. He was given the name of a young Scotsman who had returned from London where he had studied the craft of instrument-making and whose name was James Watt.

After an extensive study of the Newcomen pump Watt agreed to undertake the task of redesigning it and in 1759 commenced experiments. By 1765 he felt certain that he had worked out a change of design which would provide the increased power. At this point he had major problems to overcome before he could begin to construct an experimental model. First he was unable to find anyone in Scotland willing to finance the project, nor anyone skilled enough to undertake the precision smith-work required to build the prototype. Finally his business was in substantial debt. In all of these he was fortunate because in Roebuck he found his answers. In return for sharing the proceeds of the whole enterprise Roebuck paid off all of Watt's debts and undertook the expense of further development. He was also able to send away the smith-work, consisting of accurately machined tubes, to his contacts in the south, enabling a test model to be built.

It was 1768 before Watt was satisfied with the final design and it was patented in August of that year. The final draft of specifications and drawings for a full size model were completed in 1769.

Unfortunately Roebuck's financial affairs had taken a bad turn, he himself was ruined and his support for Watt was forced to come to an end. All was not lost, however, because in spite of his difficulties the project was saved by Roebuck once more. He introduced Watt to Mathew Boulton, one of his friends and colleagues from the Lunar Society. After close examination of all the details Boulton agreed to continue the project and finance it through to the production stage.

161

Boulton was already a very successful and wealthy Birmingham factory owner and manufacturer. He was so impressed with the possibilities that in addition to underwriting the project he made Watt a partner in his company. Henceforth known as Boulton & Watt the business went on to become even more famous.

There is no doubt that the efforts of these three men added further impetus to the Industrial Revolution. The increased power of this type of steam engine meant it could be used in many more applications. Sadly John Roebuck, whose need initiated the project, did not share in its eventual success.

John Smeaton, 1724–1792

Smeaton completely changed the method of lighthouse construction when he was entrusted with the building of the Eddystone lighthouse in 1755. The first lighthouses built on Eddystone Rock were made from timber. They could not withstand the violent sea conditions and were washed away after a few years. The second lighthouse succumbed to fire, no doubt as a result of the primitive method of illumination. The beginning of modern lighthouse construction was achieved by Smeaton in the Eddystone lighthouse which he completed in 1759, using a system of interlocking dovetailed blocks, similar to the joints in joinery, which imparted immense strength to the structure. As a binding he devised and used an improved form of cement called hydrated lime. The lighthouse stood until 1882 when it was replaced by a new structure on another part of the rocky outcrop. It appears that the need for the reconstruction arose because the rocks forming the foundations of the previous lighthouse had become unstable.

Among his other great works was the construction of the Forth and Clyde Canal in Scotland (35 miles long), which connected the Atlantic Ocean with the North Sea.

Mathew Boulton, 1728–1809

As one of the richest and most successful of the Midlands' industrialists, inventor, engineer and entrepreneur Mathew Boulton invented machinery for the manufacture of inlaid steel buckles, buttons and watch chains. In 1762 he purchased a large section of a barren heathland named Soho, close to Birmingham, where he built a large factory which incorporated a school for the study of mechanical design.

He too was closely connected with the Lunar Society, a group of men with a mutual interest in new inventions or the improvement of those already in existence. By agreement he took over from Roebuck the financial and development responsibilities for the steam pump. He had the skilled men, the machinery and the facilities to carry the project to completion. To achieve this he formed a company in 1775 called Boulton & Watt, which was highly successful in supplying all types of industry with more efficient steam power. The new company concentrated on developing steam engines to drive rotating machinery more efficiently. In this they were highly successful.

Joseph Bramah, 1749–1814

Bramah invented banknote printing machines, thief-proof locks and the hydrostatic press. His work required the development of complicated machine tool-making, as a result of which he was largely responsible for this becoming a major part of Britain's industrial base. Great inventors and innovators such as Maudslay, Wilkinson and Whitworth learned under his supervision while working for him.

Henry Greathead, 1757–1816

Greathead designed and patented the first lifeboat in 1789. He was rewarded by Parliament with the sum of £1,200 for this invaluable means of saving life at sea.

Jonathan Carter Hornblower, 1753–1815

Hornblower was the inventor of the double-beat valve, the first reciprocating compound steam engine, which he patented in 1781. With two cylinders it was vastly more efficient than its predecessors. This power, in contrast to others, made it ideally suited to the development of the locomotive and the steam boat. He was later challenged in court by Boulton & Watt for infringement of patent and had to discontinue the project over what he claimed to be a minor technicality.

Samuel Slater, 1768–1835

Slater worked in the cotton and textile industry in England where he gained valuable knowledge and experience in the spinning of cotton and also of the complex machinery which had been developed by the English inventors for large-scale textile production.

He emigrated to New England where he constructed machinery which was an exact duplication of that developed by Arkwright, and with the appropriate financial backing was instrumental in founding the American cotton industry.

It is unlikely that he could have accomplished this engineering feat from memory; therefore he must have either secretly made detailed drawings while in the employ of Arkwright's company or stolen existing plans.

His contribution to the American and local economy and

general success was such that the town of Slatersville, Rhode Island, was named after him.

Henry Maudslay, 1771–1831

Maudslay is generally regarded as the father of the machine tool industry. He invented the earliest machine tool which was the metal turning lathe. It was a general tool which could be used for the turning, boring, surfacing and screw-cutting of metal. This development enabled work of great accuracy to be achieved. He devised a system of coordinating a selection of gears by means of which a selection of precision threads could be produced with different pitches. This provided a range of threaded parts for either heavy or fine work. A further result of this invention was that it could be used to make parts for the construction of other machines to be used in a variety of manufacturing processes.

George Stephenson, 1781–1848

Stephenson was the founder of the railway system and as a consequence he changed the lives of people throughout the world.

A self-educated man, chiefly in the science of mechanics, he rose from being an assistant to his father, who was a colliery fireman, to being entrusted by Lord Ravensworth to build a travelling engine for use on the colliery tramway.

Upon completion of this in 1814 he then proceeded the following year to improve even further the engine efficiency by developing the steam-blast principle.

His next project was to build an improved locomotive for the Stockton and Tees railway which was opened in 1825. He was later commissioned to construct the Liverpool and

Manchester railway. The locomotive named 'The Rocket' reached 29 miles an hour in trial.

John Blenkinsop, 1783–1831

Blenkinsop designed the first practicable locomotive to be put into service. In 1811 he invented and patented a rack railway principally for hauling coal. It was said to be able, with an equivalent engine, to pull a load approximately five times heavier than the engine invented by Trevithick.

Another of his inventions was to fit a cogwheel to the locomotive which, when in motion, engaged with teeth that were cast on to the side of the rails. This technique is used for mountain railways.

Thomas Hancock, 1786–1865

Founder of the British rubber industry. His chief invention came in 1821 with a machine which he called the 'masticator', which could shred rubber pieces into an emulsified mass. It could then be made either into blocks or rolled into sheets similar to cloth.

He formed a partnership with a Scottish chemist by the name of Charles Macintosh who was interested in making waterproof garments from the sheet material. Unfortunately, the stitching process used by Macintosh meant that the seams were perforated, thereby admitting moisture at these points. Some way had to be found to overcome this problem. It was not until Alex Parkes arrived with his invention, which obviated the need to stitch the seams, that this problem was overcome.

Robert Stephenson, 1803–1859

Stephenson made many improvements to the 'Rocket'. He built the first Birmingham to London railway between 1833 and 1838. He designed and built the Victoria Bridge over the St Lawrence river at Montreal and also the Menai tubular bridge. He is buried with honour in Westminster Abbey.

Joseph Whitworth, 1803–1887

Whitworth introduced a method of providing a range of standardised screw-threaded parts of precision and uniformity. This readily available stock and supply of identical nuts and bolts of varying sizes was a boon to engineers during the feverish activity at the time of the Industrial Revolution.

Prior to this innovation a manufacturer of machinery was obliged to produce parts individually for each separate job. This presented the client with an unwanted delay until a replacement part could be produced. Unsurprisingly, by providing a service like this, which accelerated production with applications in every level of industrial manufacture, Whitworth became a very rich man.

He also invented the 'Whitworth gun', which was exported to America and some European countries.

As the originator of the process of 'fluid pressed steel' he added to his successes. This process was valuable for producing both cannon and ship's plates. Little wonder that he was the star of the show at the Great Exhibition in 1851.

William George Armstrong, 1810–1900

Armstrong trained initially as a solicitor. He invented the hydro-electric machine, a powerful apparatus for producing frictional electricity. Other inventions were the hydraulic crane and, in 1854, the first rifled ordnance gun. The ordnance which he designed and produced took a prominent place in the armaments of many different countries.

In addition to being an expert in hydraulic engineering, he owned the Elswick Engine Works and Shipyard on the River Tyne. Possibly as a diversion from his energetic working lifestyle, he employed some of his immense wealth to build an unusual house. Sited in Rothbury, approximately 25 miles to the north of Newcastle it was constructed in the 1880s and contained 100 rooms. Inside it reflected his genius as an inventor and innovator and many improvements were added as technology progressed. It had a lift to assist staff to convey food and fuel. A hydraulically powered spit for roasting large joints of beef was installed in the kitchen. Central heating and electric light followed. Expansive gardens and rockeries complete the setting. Now in the possession of the National Trust, it has been completely renovated and is open to the public.

Sir Henry Bessemer, 1813–1898

Sir Henry invented the process of making steel direct from pig-iron, by blowing a blast of air through it when in a state of fusion, thereby revolutionising steel manufacture. Cheap steel was then made in vast quantities and used for many purposes which its high price had previously prohibited. A steel-producing town in Alabama, USA was named in his honour for this achievement.

Alex Parkes, 1813–1890

Parkes discovered the method of cold vulcanisation and produced a material called Parkersine. In the course of his experiments at his Birmingham factory he also produced the first plastic product which he named celluloid.

Isaac Pitman, 1813–1897

Pitman invented a successful system of shorthand writing based on sound. In 1837 he published his book on the method, *Stenographic Sound Hand*.

John Brown, 1816–1896

Brown was a shipbuilder who developed a method of producing rolled steel plate which was used in the shipbuilding industry from about 1822. He also founded a shipyard on the Clyde.

John Fowler, 1817–1898

Fowler was a civil engineer of the highest calibre. He first gained experience and knowledge working for the chief engineer of the Sheffield water works. Later he worked on the London to Brighton railway. He was then appointed chief engineer on the Stockton and Hartlepool line.

In 1844 he set up as a consulting engineer with an office in London, and among the important undertakings with which he was connected was the construction of the railway system between Sheffield and Manchester.

For some years he was the engineering adviser to the viceroy of Egypt.

He designed and built Victoria Station and Pimlico Bridge, and was the first in the world to build an underground rail system. Many of these great undertakings were accomplished while he was in partnership with Benjamin Baker.

It was while in partnership with Baker, between 1882 and 1890, that these two great English engineers achieved an engineering feat of world renown and which became the pride of Scotland: the Forth Bridge.

Edward Leader Williams, 1828–1910

Leader Williams was the designer of the greatest of all British canals, the Manchester Ship Canal, a waterway for ocean-going vessels running from the estuary of the Mersey near Runcorn to Manchester, via several locks and partly in the beds of the Rivers Mersey and Irwell. The canal was begun in 1887 and completed in 1894. In the process of this huge project Leader Williams had to redesign and build an aqueduct to replace the one already positioned over the Irwell, described earlier. The aqueduct was, however, not merely a replacement but of a radically different design. It was unique in that it had to contain a section of the canal built by Brindley and then after the lock gates of the section were securely closed it had to swivel. This suspended traffic along the upper enclosed section but provided space for the seagoing ships on the canal below to pass along inland. Once the larger vessel has passed the procedure was reversed and traffic resumed on the upper part.

When the new canal was built it had a length of a little under 36 miles, an average width at the top of 172 feet while the minimum depth was 28 feet. It also had large docks at Manchester and Salford, of 71 and 33 acres respectively, which could accommodate large ships. The total cost of the undertaking was over £15 million, a massive investment in the nineteenth century.

This begs the question as to why it was deemed necessary to engage in such an enterprise by making an inland city into a large port. The answer lies in the fact that as the cotton capital Manchester was importing colossal quantities of this commodity, all of which had to be landed at the nearest large sea port, which was Liverpool. This presented Liverpool with a commercial opportunity and the city began to tax each consignment as it arrived. The Manchester merchants and manufacturers together with the City Corporation, who were large shareholders, made a decision to dig this waterway and to not only bypass Liverpool and the port taxes, but additionally to eliminate further transport costs by bringing the supplies of raw cotton in shiploads direct into the city centre. Manchester continued as a large port for about 150 years.

Benjamin Baker, 1840–1907

Baker was the chief designer and (with John Fowler) builder of the Forth Bridge in Scotland. He was also assistant (and partner) to Fowler on bridge and underground railway construction in London. He acted as consultant and adviser, offering expertise to American construction companies in both bridge building and tunnelling. From 1898 to 1902 he was responsible for the building of the Aswan Dam in the upper Nile Valley, working to the plan of William Willcock. The dam provided an immense source of hydroelectric power for Egypt.

Charles Algernon Parsons, 1854–1931

Parsons was the inventor of the steam turbine which increased dramatically engine motive power, making sensational speeds, especially following the inclusion of the screw propeller, and hastened marine development. The massive power of the turbine enabled even bigger ships to be constructed for both passenger- and cargo-carrying. Its military possibilities made it of special importance to the Admiralty.

Richard Hadfield, 1858–1940

Hadfield was a metallurgist who in 1883 discovered manganese steel, the first alloy to combine great hardness with ductility. His invention brought him recognition from every steel-producing country. He also discovered silicon and other special alloy steels.

Frederick Richard Simms, 1863–1944

Simms was the inventor of magneto ignition (with Bosch) and generally acknowledged as the father of the British motor industry as a result of demonstrating the internal combustion engine on a Thames launch in 1891, having been refused permission to operate it on land. He produced one of the first British cars, 'The Simms 2.5 Horseless Carriage' and also played an influential part in having the Light Locomotives Act of 1896 passed. This raised the permitted speed limit to 12 mph and also removed the need for a man to walk in front of a road vehicle with a red flag. In November of that year the London to Brighton Run was inaugurated to celebrate this Act. He invented the Simms coupling for matching gears, an automatic ticket-issuing machine, and also an early lawn mower.

Charles Stuart Rolls, 1877–1910, Frederick Henry Royce, 1863–1933

Rolls and Royce were two men with hugely contrasting backgrounds who somehow combined their talents to build and market a motor car of such excellence that its very name entered the vernacular to exemplify something of the very highest quality: Rolls-Royce.

Charles Stuart Rolls was born into the aristocracy. Possessed of an adventurous nature, he attained success as a racing driver and after retiring from the sport maintained his interest in motor cars by importing the best and most expensive, which he sold to his wealthy society contacts from his London agency. He also took up flying as an interest.

Frederick Henry Royce arrived by a much harder and more circuitous route. Many of his early jobs were aimed at little more than survival and were preceded by minimal formal education. In spite of these shortcomings he embarked on an almost relentless quest of self-study which included electrics, mathematics and – in view of his later career – must also have encompassed mechanical drawing. Because of his almost obsessive interest in all things mechanical he seems to have acquired some skills in the use of machine tools, probably through contact with people of similar interests.

His interest in electrics proved to be his saviour because he managed to obtain work in London for a company of electrical factors with whom he later obtained promotion to their branch office in Lancashire. From there he gained both experience and contacts and with one of the people he met he set up in partnership, making electrical goods.

Based on his now more secure background, Royce began to turn his attention to motor cars, one of the major obsessions of the early 1900s. After casting an eye over the models on sale at the time, most of which he regarded as 'boneshakers' he built one of his own which, though small compared to the foreign models of the time, more than compensated by its smooth and silent performance.

The intention of Royce was to build bigger and better cars than those on the market at that time. As many people have found out in business, however, the problems of finance and efficient marketing are difficult obstacles to overcome, especially in the initial stages of a company, no matter how good the product.

Fortunately one party was so impressed with the quality and engineering of the car that he effected an introduction between Rolls and Royce, whose complimentary abilities and belief in excellence produced a vehicle which won the admiration of the motoring world. During the Second World War the company went on to produce the finest aircraft engines in the world.

Reginald Joseph Mitchell, 1895–1937

This outstanding engineer set new standards for aviation design with his sleek monoplane shape, which emerged from his experience gained in designing planes for competition in the Schneider Cup races. In the period just after the First World War interest in aviation increased partly because it was realised just how important a part it could play in support of the military. Mitchell's curiosity and ingenuity were prompting him to explore the limits to which flight could be taken.

Early Schneider races were won by the American military and later by the Curtiss company, but as a result of the brilliant designs of Mitchell, England won the trophy outright in 1931 with the Supermarine 6B, which reached speeds of over 400 mph.

Mitchell later designed the Spitfire fighter plane which played such a vital part in the Battle of Britain and especially so when it was allied to the Rolls-Royce Merlin engine designed by Frank Whittle.

Considering that Mitchell began his working life as an apprentice in a locomotive works the extent of his achievements is truly astonishing.

Frank Whittle, 1907–1996

Probably the greatest aero-engineer of the twentieth century, Whittle ensured that Britain was the first to enter the jet age when he patented his invention of the jet engine on 16 January 1930. The jet-propelled Gloster Whittle E28/39 flew successfully from Cranwell on 15 May 1941, achieving a top speed of 370 mph at 25,000 feet and was faster than the Spitfire or any other conventional propeller-driven machine.

Although others were engaged in the race to develop such machinery, Whittle was the first to design and produce a practical engine.

His father was a very competent engineer who owned a small engineering company, thus enabling young Frank to become familiar with good engineering practice at an early age. After twice being rejected by the RAF because of his small stature, he persisted in his efforts to join, finally becoming successful at the third attempt, assisted by having undertaken a rigorous programme of physical exercise. Entry into an apprenticeship with the RAF allowed him to further his studies and later, when he won a much sought-after cadetship to the RAF College, he could increase his aeronautical knowledge by becoming a pilot. This proved to be the case and he was able to ally the practical experience gained from actually flying to the revolutionary theories which he was developing.

He remained fascinated by science and the greater possibilities in aircraft engine design. In 1928 he submitted a revolutionary paper entitled 'Future Developments in Aircraft Design'. However, a lack of support and sometimes positive obstruction from both the government and the hierarchy at the Air Ministry delayed the progress of the jet age until 1941, but once the success of this invention could no longer be denied, the authorities finally gave the go-ahead and the finance to proceed with a project which changed the face of aviation for ever.

Had the government, the military chiefs and the aviation industry of the time shared the vision of Whittle and given the proper support to his enterprise, the jet aircraft could have had an enormous impact on the Second World War and, by shortening the conflict, could have saved many lives.

Whittle was awarded a CBE in 1944, a CB in 1947, a KBE in 1948 and the United States Legion of Merit in 1946, among many other honours.

Christopher S. Cockerell, 1910–1999

Cockerell was the inventor of the hovercraft, a vehicle designed to travel on a cushion of air encased within a neoprene skirt fastened around the lower edges of the body of the vehicle and providing the necessary lift. It lends itself to a variety of uses as it can travel over deep or shallow water and even over marshland or sand. Cockerell held a patent for a number of inventions, one of which was an aviation direction finder.

Lionel Alexander Bethune Pilkington, 1920–1995

Pilkington introduced a revolutionary way of producing sheet glass without having to grind and polish the surface afterwards. This was the 'Float Glass' method which Alistair Pilkington invented and put into operation in 1959.

The Pilkington company had been founded in St Helens, Lancashire early in the nineteenth century by members of his family but it was after the invention of the 'Float' process and the great success it became, that great expansion of the company took place.

Trevor Baylis, 1937–

Trevor Baylis is a man who has always been interested in inventing, and in 1993 was watching a programme on television which dealt with the problems in Africa including AIDS and the difficulties encountered by the governments in communicating with people in isolated rural areas. Radio was the only means of contact but even if available the people could not always afford to buy the batteries to operate one.

A solution was needed which did not rely on the conventional provision of electricity. Baylis experimented with a small radio, an electric motor and a hand brace. He discovered that by turning the motor by means of the brace he could generate enough electricity to power the radio. He then deduced that by substituting a coiled spring for the brace and fitting a winding mechanism, this could release energy in the same way as a clock mechanism is driven.

The result was his invention of the clockwork radio.

The South African government found the means to distribute these sets among the villages and millions of disadvantaged people were given contact with the outside world, many for the first time. Even those who could afford battery-operated models were relieved of the cost of batteries which to them were not easily affordable.

10

Medical Pioneers

Since ancient times people have tried to find ways of treating disease. It has been said that the origins of primitive medicine were a form of white magic. If it worked it meant that there was a precedent from which a conclusion could be drawn to be used should a similar circumstance arise. The Greeks were the earliest to remove medical observation from folklore and the supernatural and were followed by the school at Padua, Italy where Harvey, one of the greatest names in seventeenth-century medicine, studied. Some who came after and added their contribution are listed below.

William Harvey, 1578–1657

Harvey studied at Cambridge and then at Padua, Italy, in what was then considered the most celebrated school of medicine in Europe. Returning to London he became the elected physician at St Bartholomew's Hospital. He deciphered the mystery of the circulation of blood in the body. His findings on the subject were formally published in Amsterdam in 1628. In doing so he declared that he had, for at least nine years, demonstrated, lectured and taught the principles of his theory. Although his views were attacked by some foreign physicians they were soon fully accepted by the wider medical authorities.

179

Benjamin Jesty, 1736–1816

Although Edward Jenner is nowadays given the credit for the introduction of vaccination against smallpox, the acknowledgement is not entirely accurate. Indeed, he was responsible for its acceptance throughout the medical world but events proved him not to be the original discoverer.

Jenner seemingly became interested in the subject after hearing it being discussed by country folk where he was practising, but he was not aware that this was as a result of the procedure having already taken place within the region.

It was only after vaccination had become universally recognised and publicised that Benjamin Jesty came forward. He was able to prove conclusively that he had used the same methods and achieved identical results in treating people some 20 years earlier. The government unreservedly accepted the evidence and in recognition of his work presented him with a long testimonial, a pair of gold-mounted lancets and commissioned a portrait to be painted.

Edward Jenner, 1749–1823

Jenner is celebrated for the discovery and introduction of the practice of vaccination as a preventative of smallpox.

After studying surgery and anatomy he finally decided to return to his native county of Gloucestershire to become a medical practitioner.

About 1776 he began to take a specific interest in the subject of smallpox, a terrible disease with a high mortality rate, more so in countries with a hot climate. Even those who survived were usually very badly scarred, especially on the face. There is also a simpler type of this disease known as cowpox which is not so virulent and can be transmitted from the animal to the person doing the milking.

In the area where he lived there was a general belief, presumably gained from observation, that the milkmaids who contracted the lesser form were unlikely to suffer the more virulent type. It was decided to expose willing volunteers to this infection by injecting them with this milder form.

Many years of experiments followed and once Jenner became convinced that the method was both safe and effective he then published his famous paper on the process of vaccine inoculation in 1798. The same year he introduced the practice of vaccination into St Thomas's Hospital, London.

There were those in the medical profession both at home and abroad who opposed his method, but it proved beyond doubt to be an effective preventive and was finally universally accepted.

Apart from the plaudits which he received from foreign governments and monarchs, in 1802 a parliamentary grant of £10,000 was accorded him and in 1807 a further grant of £20,000 was made. The principle of vaccination is now used throughout the world to control many other forms of contagious and infectious diseases.

Joseph Lister, 1827–1912

A very influential figure in the medical world of his time, Lister served from 1860 as Professor of Surgery at Glasgow University and later in the equivalent post in Edinburgh. His early work concentrated upon the concept of antisepsis and the results he achieved by utilising this method earned him an international reputation.

His findings were taken a step further by expounding the principle of preventing a wound being infected by bacteria during surgery. This is accepted nowadays throughout the world of medicine as being the golden rule, but he at first met with strong opposition.

He became such an integral and famous part of the medical scene in Scotland that when Bill Bryson journeyed around Britain in the latter part of the twentieth century compiling a catalogue of people and events for a book which he was researching, he mistakenly referred to him as a Scotsman.

Patrick Steptoe, 1913–1988

Steptoe was a gynaecologist and doctor who had spent much of his life engaged in medical research and in particular that of infertility. Together with his colleague Robert Edwards, who was also accomplished in the same medical field, they realised the fulfilment of their ambitions: to perfect a method of in-vitro fertilization.

In a hospital in Oldham, Lancashire, on 25 July 1978 the culmination of their ground-breaking accomplishment was witnessed by the world when Louise Brown was born. This was the first 'test-tube birth' and followed the laboratory fertilisation of the mother.

Francis Harry Compton Crick, 1916–2004

After the Second World War, where he had been engaged in the detection of mines and torpedoes, Francis Crick obtained a post at Cambridge in the Cavendish Research Laboratory. There, from 1947, he worked on biological research until in 1949, when he transferred the focus of his attention to genes, the structures of proteins and nucleic acids.

He investigated everything which might unravel the mystery of the mechanism by which children inherit their characteristics from previous generations, which the scientists described as the genetic code. After two years of intensive work he was, apparently, in possession of a great deal of information on the subject of DNA and nucleic acids, when in 1951 he was joined by another scientific researcher, James Watson, who was also intensely interested in the subject and, like Crick, prepared to totally immerse himself in the search for the genetic key which could provide the answer.

What has been described as the most earth-shattering scientific revolution of the twentieth century occurred in 1953 when Crick together with his colleague Watson announced that they had discovered the double helix structure of the molecule DNA. In doing so they had unravelled the biological secrets of life and also added a new dimension to forensic medicine with DNA fingerprinting.

Crick, Watson and Maurice Wilkins, another colleague and research contributor, were in 1962 awarded the Nobel Prize for Medicine for discovering the 'secret of life'.

Godfrey Hounsfield, 1919–2004

A brilliant and largely self-taught scientist, Hounsfield led the team which developed Britain's first solid state computer. In 1979 he was awarded the Nobel Prize for Physiology or Medicine for inventing the computerised axial tomography (CAT) scanner for use in clinical diagnosis.

He believed that by combining hundreds of X-ray beams which were directed towards a given object from differing angles, it should be possible to obtain a three-dimensional cross-sectional image. He reasoned that if this were to be applied to a human brain it would be possible to make an accurate diagnosis of its condition.

A machine was eventually constructed combining computer and X-ray technology and it was put into service in 1972. In practice, it proved that it could scan a human brain in a little over four minutes and provide detailed images. Incidentally, for the first brain scan trials Hounsfield allowed his own head to be used.

He later modified the scanner and produced another model to a larger scale enabling it to scan a complete human body. Diagnosis of diseases of the brain, body tissue or bone structure can now be made without resorting to distressing or dangerous investigative surgery.

Unbeknown to Hounsfield a nuclear physicist in South Africa had worked on similar lines and had published a paper on the subject, although he had never produced a machine in support of his work. Nevertheless, when the Nobel Prize Committee considered the invention they decided to share the Prize for the development of CAT in Physiology or Medicine between them.

Ian Wilmut, 1944–

In 1996, while working at the Roslin Institute in Scotland, this brilliant English scientist successfully produced Dolly the Sheep, the first animal to be cloned from an adult cell. Wilmut specialises in the field of genetics and the cloning of human embryos for the provision of stem cells for use in the treatment of degenerative disorders. The vast scale of his research and discoveries may take years to be fully understood and absorbed by the medical and scientific bodies to enable further development to take place.

Because of the nature of this biological research there are moral and ethical questions to be answered and professional bodies all over the world are examining the evidence from the legislative point of view.

Wilmut enjoys a distinguished career as a scientist and biological researcher. He attended the University of Nottingham where he obtained a BSc in agricultural science and later the University of Cambridge where in 1971 he earned a PhD.

11

The Great and Influential

Ideas seem to be more durable than any invention, especially if they embody high ideals or visions of substance. Whether they are motivated by pity, conscience, sense of justice or self-sacrifice they remain the bedrock of human aspiration. Included in the list below are some who have left a lasting impact on history.

St Cuthbert, circa 635–687

Celebrated Father of the early English Church, his learning and holiness brought him much unsought fame. He was particularly influential in the most practical way possible by imparting knowledge of better agricultural practices to the people of Northumbria, especially in the area now known as the Lowlands of Scotland. He was revered by the Picts who resided in Galloway and the south-west of Scotland. He retired to the desolate Isle of Farne until his death.

Bede, circa 672–735

The 'Venerable Bede' was an English historian and theologian born in the neighbourhood of Monkwearmouth, County Durham.

The most learned Englishman of his day and in some sense regarded as the father of English history, Bede's most important work was his *Historia Ecclesiastical Gentis Anglorem* (*Ecclesiastical History of England*). King Alfred later translated this work into Anglo-Saxon. Bede knew Greek and Latin, and also had some knowledge of Hebrew.

St Boniface, 680–755

The apostle of Germany, whose original name was Winfrid. He was born of a noble Anglo-Saxon family. He took orders as a priest in his thirtieth year and in 718 went to Rome, after which he was authorised by Pope Gregory II to preach the Gospel to the pagans of Germany. In 723 he was made a bishop and in 732 an archbishop and primate of all Germany. Many bishoprics of Germany, such as Ratisbon, Erfurt, Paderborn, Wurzburg, together with the famous abbey of Fulda, owe their foundation to him. He was slain in West Friesland by a heathen tribe in 755 and buried in the abbey of Fulda.

Alcuin of York, 735–804

A very learned man, Alcuin was educated at York School, of which he eventually became headmaster. Later he travelled to Rome and other Continental seats of learning. Charles the Great (Charlemagne) became acquainted with him during a visit to Parma, and invited him, in 782, to his court to make use of his services as an adviser in his endeavours to civilize his subjects.

To secure the benefit of his instructions, Charlemagne established at his court a school, called *Schola Palatina*, or the Palace School. In the Royal Academy Alcuin was called

Flaccus Albinus. Most of the schools in France were either founded or improved by him. He founded the school in the Abbey of St Martin of Tours in 796 after the model of the school in York.

Although he left the court in 801 Alcuin maintained a correspondence with Charlemagne to his death in 804. He left works on theology, philosophy and rhetoric, and also poems and letters, all of which have been published.

Pope Adrian IV, 1100–1159

The only English Pope ever appointed, and originally named Nicholas Breakspear. He became abbot of St Rufus in Provence, France, and cardinal and legate to Norway. He was chosen as Pope in 1154. His tenure was marred by an almost constant struggle for supremacy against Frederick Barbarossa, the German emperor who spent a considerable part of his life trying to subjugate the Italian city states.

William Caxton, 1422–1491

This unusual man deserves special mention. He brought the written word 'in English' within the grasp of everyone. He was originally apprenticed to Robert Large, a London mercer. Upon the death of his master Caxton went into business for himself in Bruges. His influence grew, which led to him being appointed (circa 1463) governor at Bruges to the London Association of Merchant Adventurers. In 1471 he also entered the service of Margaret, Duchess of Burgundy, sister of Edward IV.

He became associated with the newly-discovered art of printing and his *Recuyell of the Historyes Troye*, the translation of a popular mediaeval romance (from the French of Raoul le Fevre) was printed about 1474, probably at Bruges, and is the earliest specimen of typography in the English language.

His *Game and Playe of the Chesse* (Bruges 1475) is the second English book printed.

In 1476 he returned to England and set up his printing works in Westminster. In 1477 he printed Lord River's translation of *The Dictes and Sayengis of the Philosophres*, the first book actually printed in England. In 14 years he printed approximately 80 books, many going into two or three editions.

He translated 21 books from the French, mainly romances, and one (*Reynard the Fox*) from the Dutch. In doing so he helped materially to fix the literary language.

Besides these works he also printed Chaucer's *Canterbury Tales*, *Troylus and Cressida*, Mallory's *Morte D'Arthur* and the *Fables* of Aesop.

He was patronised by Edward IV, Richard III and Henry VII, and at least two noblemen translated works for his press.

Thomas Cranmer, 1489–1556

Cranmer was Archbishop of Canterbury and noted for the part he played in the Reformation during the reign of Henry VIII.

Upon the accession of Mary he was arrested for his part in supporting Lady Jane Grey. Refusing to recant he became a Protestant martyr when Mary Tudor ordered him to be burned at the stake at Oxford.

He was responsible for the translation of the Bible into English and also the *Book of Common Prayer*.

Oliver Cromwell, 1599–1658

Possibly the most significant event affecting English (and British) social and governmental progress since the Norman Conquest was the advent of this man and his place in the momentous happenings of his lifetime. He certainly emerged as the pivotal figure during the Civil War and its aftermath.

The English Civil War is in itself a misnomer because the central figure in it was a Scottish king (Charles I) whose misrule and adherence to the idea of divine right of kingship was the central cause of the conflict. It was the determination of Charles to enforce his right to rule without the consent of Parliament which caused him to set in motion a chain of events which made war unavoidable. He began his reign by attempting to impose taxes without the agreement of Parliament. This resulted in strong resistance and a stalemate, whereupon he dissolved the House and repeated the action until after the third time he decided to rule without a Parliament. He did so with the help of two advisers and using the courts of the High Commission and the Star Chamber to enforce his arbitrary laws.

Even his coronation, which took place in Edinburgh in 1633 with full Anglican ceremonial, upset many of his fellow Scots. Furthermore, it was his attempt to introduce an Anglican liturgy into Scotland which met with violent and warlike opposition and gave origin to the Covenant in 1638 opposing it. He then declared war on his own people and sent a punitive force north, but they were defeated by the Covenanters.

The next phase of dispute began between the king and his aristocratic supporters together with the bulk of the gentry. They were opposed by the Puritans who were allied to the inhabitants of the major trading towns. The immutable ideology separating the two sides culminated in both preparing for war.

The details of the ensuing Civil War are best followed by

the accounts given by numerous learned historians, but from that day forward the king and Cromwell became implacable enemies

As far as Cromwell is concerned it would be folly to attempt to encapsulate in a few words a life of such magnitude and which was so multi-faceted. Many accomplished historians have addressed the task and dealt with the many aspects of his life successfully. Others have taken a narrower view and remain purely political or subjective. Accounts written during the period immediately following the Restoration can be discounted for obvious reasons.

It is difficult to accept, without question, the invective sometimes directed at Cromwell. He reflected the mood of the nation, and defended the right of the democratic parliamentary system for which the English, over centuries, had shed much blood to establish.

There is no doubt that the Stuarts, who had an extremely close affinity with the French court and its royal practices, chose to emulate them and in so doing exhibited almost total ignorance of the English character.

The social and political upheaval of this period took a long time to heal but eventually left a legacy which set the model for modern constitutional monarchy the world over, and in doing so preserved the concept for many countries other than our own.

It should be remembered that Cromwell achieved this without allowing the situation to become out of control, as was the case in France following their revolution and the subsequent indiscriminate bloodletting during the 'Terror'.

Some measure of the continuing malign attitudes of King Charles II and his supporters of the time may be gleaned from the fact that even after the Restoration their bitterness was not assuaged. That they had Cromwell's body exhumed and hanged on a gibbet at Tyburn and his head fixed to a pole at Westminster Abbey speaks volumes.

On the subject of Cromwell it seems difficult to disentangle fact from fiction and justice from aristocratic self-interest, especially for the layman.

John Harvard, 1607–1638

Born in Southwark, London, where he first attended school, Harvard went on to graduate from Cambridge University. In 1637 he went to America and became a minister of a church in Charleston, which has now been absorbed by the city of Boston, Massachusetts.

He had apparently been party to discussions directed to the founding of a college within the region, and when the following year he died he bequeathed his entire library, which was of some significance, plus half his property, to the project. This enabled the college to be built and by 1642 they had awarded the first graduation certificate.

Harvard is the oldest university in what is now the USA and was named after its benefactor. Harvard University now enjoys an unrivalled worldwide reputation.

Memorials to John Harvard can be found in Southwark Cathedral and Stratford-upon-Avon.

Elihu Yale, 1649–1721

Yale's donations paved the way for an ordinary college which was under financial constraints to realise its ambitions and become a great educational institution.

It is the third oldest university in the USA.

Yale made his fortune during his time working for the East India Company in Madras, and although he retired to London he had many colonial contacts through which he made many endowments.

John Wesley, 1703–1791

Wesley's brand of worship took place with a small number of friends initially, but the simplicity of his preaching had great appeal and he was invited to America in 1735 to preach to the colonists of Georgia.

He travelled almost unceasingly and would ride 40–60 miles a day to meet his commitments. The principles of episcopalianism were always firmly held by him and he never sought to formally separate from the Church of England.

Samuel Johnson, 1709–1784

Lexicographer, scholar, parliamentary reporter, author and playwright, Johnson began work on his famous dictionary in 1747, the plan of which he had announced the same year. It was regarded at the time as a significant work but has long since been superseded. Although one of the best known literary figures of his time, his works are seldom read today. An excellent biography of his life was written by his friend James Boswell.

John Newton, 1725–1807

In 1764 Newton was the writer of arguably the most moving of all Christian hymns, 'Amazing Grace'. He led an extraordinary life having been press-ganged on to a ship. For years he found himself engaged in the slave trade and leading a dissolute and profligate existence until finally touching rock bottom. He eventually escaped, and experiencing self-disgust sought solace in religion, subsequently being ordained an Anglican priest.

Thomas Paine, 1737–1809

Undoubtedly Paine inspired American thinking on the subject of independence, particularly its eventual founders. His writings had an enormous influence at a time when English colonists in America were becoming exasperated with the British government, which imposed taxes upon them, while at the same time denying them a voice in Parliament.

He had an unquenchable desire to improve the way royal governments of the world treated their subjects. He was particularly appalled at what he saw as the total disregard by the ruling classes in Britain of their own people. His writing mirrored his disgust and severely alarmed the British government which feared the impact it could have on a population already disaffected with their living conditions and clamouring for more say in the country's affairs in general. The government was especially fearful that the burgeoning unrest in France, which later gathered impetus and culminated in revolution, might spread to Britain. Paine had given considerable support to the French cause and his writing had inspired them.

The practicality of his arguments made a great impact both at home and abroad. In particular, social injustice and the lack of equality was the general theme of his pamphlet entitled 'Common Sense'. It supported the English colonists in America, clearly analysing the faults of the British government of the time.

Afterwards he issued another pamphlet called 'The Crisis' in which he reinforced his opinions, providing explicit and cogent reasons, why America should look further than just to claim the right to play a more influential role in a partnership with Great Britain; he suggested they should go for outright independence. They could then conjoin their states as a legislative body, execute their own laws and use their taxes as they saw fit. In 1787, after his return to England, Paine wrote *The Rights of Man* which again offended the establishment and a prosecution was begun against him. However, he escaped to France.

The views he had expressed in his various papers attracted numerous admirers in France and he was invited to become a member of the National Convention of the Department of Calais. Though he despised monarchy and all it stood for, at the trial of Louis XVI he voted against the death penalty, proposing instead imprisonment to be followed by banishment. Like most civilised people he was sickened by the barbarity of those revolutionary powers then in charge of France.

This attitude offended the Jacobins and in 1793 he was removed from the Convention, arrested and imprisoned. He was fortunate to escape the guillotine.

Another inflammatory work called *The Age of Reason* was published about this time in both Paris and London and ensured that he would be risking at least his liberty should he dare to return to England. In all of these works Paine railed against the Americas any longer being ruled by Britain. He was friendly with both Benjamin Franklin and Thomas Jefferson, with whom he exchanged opinions frequently. The latter was much influenced by Paine's works when he drew up the American Constitution.

William Wilberforce, 1759–1833

Wilberforce's persistent campaigning brought an end to slave traders importing slaves from Africa to the British colonies. He first asked the government for leave to bring in a Bill to prevent the practice in 1791 but it was consistently defeated until 1807, during the short period of the administration of Charles Fox, Secretary for Foreign Affairs. Slavery was then made illegal under British law and applied to the conveyance of slaves anywhere in the world.

Wilberforce then concentrated his efforts to bring about the total abolition of the slave trade, and the Act of 1807, which imposed fines on anyone breaking the law. It was strengthened in 1811 to incur imprisonment, which was more of a deterrent.

It should be noted that Wilberforce was not alone in his quest. He had in Thomas Clarkson a powerful and energetic ally with whom in 1787 he had founded a society for the suppression of the slave trade. The two men next directed their energies toward the emancipation of the existing slaves in the British Empire and with help from other influential sympathisers brought into being the Emancipation Act of 1833, abolishing slavery throughout the Empire. Slave-owners were given compensation. France took a similar step in 1843 and Holland in 1863. Almost simultaneously the Spanish colonies in South America revolted and set up their own republics, accompanied by the abolition of slavery. This left only Brazil, which did not abolish slavery until 1888, and the USA.

In the southern states of the USA dependence on slave labour had created such large vested interests that slavery continued to be maintained and defended. In 1860 it is estimated that there were almost 4 million slaves in the American southern states.

The abolition of the practice did not occur until after the termination of the Civil War in 1865. It was not abolished in Nepal until 1926.

Thomas Clarkson, 1760–1846

An avid emancipationist even during his student days at Cambridge University, Clarkson allied himself with, and possibly inspired, Wilberforce and the Quakers in their fight against slavery.

While Wilberforce argued the case in Parliament, Clarkson conducted the campaign throughout England and France. His efforts were a major factor in persuading public opinion everywhere to condemn the practice and his contribution to securing the prohibition of the slave trade was immense.

Slavery and the Slave Trade

A particularly shameful episode in this abhorrent practice began with the discovery of the New World in the fifteenth century. Previous entries describe those so offended by it that they spent their lives campaigning to bring it to an end.

The practice of slavery was common throughout ancient times, although there was a distinction between actual slavery and bondage. The latter could be brought about by incurring debt or as a punishment for a crime.

Ancient Greek civilisation has many admirers but their society, like that of the Romans, was built on slavery. Aristotle defended their actions on the grounds that some people were 'slaves by nature' and could be happy and useful only in a condition of dependence.

Early Roman treatment of slaves was generally very cruel and led to the formidable revolt led by Spartacus (circa 73 BC). This, though, was merely an isolated incident and did not arrest the taking of slaves by the Romans for hundreds of years.

Arab slave traders operated in North Africa for centuries before that. They were also actively engaged in raiding European ports for their victims.

Spain, Portugal, France, Britain and other colonial powers engaged in the slave trade, using slaves to work on the plantations as a means of exploiting the riches to be found in the New World. This is probably the most shameful chapter in modern history.

Equally shameful is the fact that it is extremely unlikely that the slavery of the eighteenth and nineteenth centuries could have existed on such a scale had the African tribal chiefs not been so willing to sell their tribesmen and women to the slave traders.

Slavery was not confined to one race or section of the world. Thousands of Christian slaves were held in captivity in Algiers, and in 1816 the British fleet under Lord Exmouth bombarded the city to ensure their release.

Elizabeth Fry, 1780–1845

Fry was a social reformer, horrified by the conditions in English prisons. She harangued the government of the day to act more humanely towards those who were incarcerated, sometimes for minor offences, in the most appalling conditions.

A visit to Newgate prison in 1813 was the catalyst which sparked off her campaign, when she concluded that punishment need not be accompanied by the squalor and general degradation which she encountered. From that time onwards she dedicated herself to helping the unfortunate women suffering such treatment.

Her first success came with the establishment of a ladies committee for the reformation of women prisoners in Newgate, with school facilities, and also extending to what would nowadays be termed 'occupational therapy' which engaged the prisoners in the manufacture of basic products.

The authorities were obviously impressed with the results because Fry was soon allowed to introduce these changes into other prisons. Eventually she was invited to France, Belgium, Germany and Holland to talk about her ideas.

Richard Doyle, 1824–1883

Boyle designed the cover for the first issue of the magazine *Punch* and also invented the idea of the comic strip cartoon which he based on the activities of a riding school around 1850.

Punch has long enjoyed a reputation for humour, satire and ridicule aimed at the pompous in society and at that time provided a new vehicle for this purpose.

Grace Darling, 1815–1842

This remarkable heroine was born in the Longstone lighthouse on the Farne Islands off the coast of Northumberland. Her father William was the lighthouse keeper. In 1838, the steamer *Forfarshire*, carrying 41 passengers plus crew members, became disabled during a storm off the Farne Islands. After being thrown against a rock the boat broke in two, leaving some of the passengers and crew clinging to part of the wreck.

They were about a mile away from the lighthouse when they were first seen by William Darling at daylight the following morning.

With only a small rowing boat at his disposal he seriously doubted if it would be possible to attempt a rescue, especially in such a violent sea. His intrepid daughter implored her father to take the risk and to allow her to accompany him. He reluctantly agreed and each taking an oar they reached the wreck and succeeded in rescuing nine survivors.

The news of this outstanding act of selfless bravery spread, and a public subscription of £750 was raised. Unfortunately this intrepid spirit was quenched within four years when she died from consumption. It is distinctly possible that this disease could have had its beginnings in the severe exposure which she must have endured on that fateful day.

Thomas Cook, 1818–1892

Cook was the first travel agent to organise trips to many different countries. He began in about 1841 by chartering a train to convey a group to a meeting in the Midlands of England. He later took the idea a step further and entered the mass holiday market by offering holidays to larger numbers of people to various destinations in Europe. Although he inspired many imitators to join what has become a major industry in providing affordable holidays both at home and abroad, his company has continued to be one of the leaders within the industry.

Florence Nightingale, 1820–1910

From an early age Florence Nightingale exhibited an interest in the relief of human suffering and visited the chief military hospitals in Europe to study the nursing methods and systems.

During the Crimean War (1854–1856) she was appalled at the low standards of the hospitals and care. She offered to organise a team of highly trained nurses to go to Scutari to tend the sick and wounded. The government accepted her offer and arranged for the group to travel to the war region. She and her assistants gave great service to the soldiery and relieved a great deal of suffering. Her own dedicated and incessant work, then and later, when she embarked on a strenuous programme of hospital reform, caused her to suffer a breakdown in health.

In recognition of her services, the sum of £50,000 was raised by public subscription and presented to her. Her immediate and unselfish reaction was to use it as a fund to create an institution, attached to St Thomas's Hospital, London, for the training of nurses.

William 'General' Booth, 1829–1912

Booth was educated privately and was for some time a preacher among the Wesleyan Methodists, but decided to devote himself to general evangelistic work. In 1865 he began a mission in the East End of London, which in 1878 assumed the name of the Salvation Army. It has since become an organisation carrying on its labours all over the world and the name has become synonymous with the amelioration of the conditions of the poor, disadvantaged, degraded and destitute throughout the world. This humane work is still continuing in the twenty-first century.

John Henry Newman, 1801–1890

A revered thinker and theologian, Newman was the rector of Dublin University from 1854 to 1858. He wrote 'Lead Kindly Light', and the great narrative poem *The Dream of Gerontius*.

Edith Cavell, 1865–1915

In her vocation as a nurse Cavell attained the highest reputation and in 1907 was appointed matron of the Ecole Belge d'Infirmieres Diplomees Brussels. Upon the outbreak of the First World War she felt unable to return to the safety of England and remained in Brussels during the German invasion to help to care for the wounded. Stemming from her compulsion to assist the injured, sick or wounded, she harboured French, Belgian and British soldiers in her house, some of whom made their escape from Belgium and the Germans.

The German military commandant had her arrested and charged with assisting the enemy. She did not deny the charges, in fact she openly confessed, and for this in the early morning of the 12 October 1915 she was shot by firing squad.

The execution of this sentence sent a wave of revulsion throughout the civilised world. The secretary of the American legation had tried to intercede on her behalf, pleading for leniency, but the German military governor, Baron von Bissing, would not be moved and insisted that the sentence be carried out.

A statue of her was erected in London between St Martin's Church and the National Gallery, and was unveiled in 1920 by Queen Alexandra.

12

On Character and Generalisation

The English

One wonders if any other nation has been so subjected to such critical observation and analysis as the English. Over the years numerous books and articles have appeared, some castigating them for their faults and others praising their virtues. Like people of any nation or community they are neither as good nor as bad as sometimes perceived by their critics, admirers or even themselves. Perhaps this abnormal interest arises from a sense of surprise that a country so small has made such an impact on the world. An opening gambit, often used in surveys on the subject is, 'What is your opinion of the English?' Any question based on such a weak premise is bound to elicit that weakest of all responses generalisation! Only one question registers lower than this on the idiocy scale and that is – 'What does being English mean to you?' The trouble is that many of the people who burst into print claiming to have discovered the secret of the English character then go on to produce an article based on vacuous generalities or apocryphal stories. One of the earlier classic generalisations was made by Napoleon in answer to the first of these questions, when he stated dismissively, 'The English are a nation of shopkeepers'. Did he ever stop to wonder who was looking after their shops while they were delivering to the French at Agincourt, Crecy, Poitiers and Sluys and, more particularly in his case, Waterloo? Perhaps he assumed that the battles all coincided with half-day closing.

Just examine a few more of the criticisms which have been made of the English occasionally from those who, in the guise of academics or intuitive journalists, state accusingly 'The English are unimaginative' or 'The English do not respect intellectuals'. Comparisons with other nations are made or quotes are unearthed from foreign sources to prove a point. One is forced to admit that, as far as the appreciation of purely academic thinkers is concerned, they are right, the English do display such scepticism. The application of common sense, or the value of study with a tangible objective, is more highly regarded than purely speculative thought. There is, however, justifiable suspicion towards some intellectuals and their behaviour in the past. From among the intelligentsia, beneficiaries of the finest education and lifestyle that could be enjoyed, were people such as Guy Burgess, Donald McLean, Anthony Blunt and Kim Philby, who became spies for a foreign government. Their brand of deep thinking was to explore subversive ways of betraying the country which had nurtured them while at the same time enjoying the fruits of high office. Others were from the Oxford Union, whose members once cast a vote stating that they would not fight for king and country.

An undeniable characteristic of the English is one of tolerance, which they sometimes carry to the point where it becomes a weakness. They are also inclined to self parody and self denigration among themselves but usually as a form of humour, exaggerated from a thread of fact.

Even those considered to be learned people can become extravagant generalisers when writing about the English. One well-known author purports to have carefully analysed the English character and engages the reader's attention initially by tabling the premise that 'the English are almost unlovable'.

He then goes on to list the attractive and enviable qualities possessed by the Irish, Welsh and Scots. This, though, is only the beginning of his exercise in generalisation of Olympian proportions which anyone possessing a smidgen of rationale must dismiss with a shake of the head. The diatribe goes on to say that even those English people who are polite are, in being so, only expressing a form of contempt. One can imagine the outcry if statements like these were made about the Jews or any other social group or nationality residing in the United Kingdom. In my opinion this pushes English tolerance beyond the acceptable limit. One must feel sympathy for someone with such views. If they are 'genuinely' held it cannot be easy for the holder to continue to live in England.

Every year I watch with admiration the televising of the London, Manchester and Gateshead marathons, as well as the Great North Run, when almost a couple of hundred thousand English men and women put themselves through agony to raise large amounts of money for their favourite charitable causes. They cover as far as 26 miles, sometimes in the most outlandish and uncomfortable costumes, and not always in the best of weather. Their endeavours are supported by thousands of friends from pubs, clubs, offices and neighbourhoods who sponsor them financially Can these people be of the same nation so deprecatingly described by our acerbic writer as 'unlovable' hypocrites? Perhaps, for the purpose of his book, the writer in question was only spoofing.

It has been said in recent years that 'the English have lost their national identity', usually by some hack short of ideas for an article required by his or her paper. What rubbish! To an English person nationality is something which they regard as an accepted fact, not open to question, nor deemed necessary to have it continually re-affirmed. It is not something to be brandished like a weapon, as some blatantly do. If interviewed on the subject English people tend to treat the question as pointless and unnecessary. This reluctance to elaborate on the subject is possibly why it is fatuously construed as not having a national identity. Even the prospect of being required to have an identity card is regarded as an unwarranted intrusion.

'The English do not have a national dress' declare some of the more myopically challenged! Without question the most popular male mode of dress in the western world and beyond, is what is known as the 'lounge suit'. This garment, when properly worn, is practical, functional and elegant. The wearing of it is not restricted and it need not be overly expensive. Where did it originate? It was designed and produced by the English – Saville Row in London being its Temple – to where the rich and famous from all over the world still come to worship its excellence. So, to those of you who are not English, you do not have to engage in some arcane search of your ancestors before being granted leave to wear it.

Furthermore on the subject of fashion and style, the father of international haute couture was an Englishman – Charles Edward Worth. In the latter part of the nineteenth century he opened his House of Fashion in Paris. The first of its type. He devoted himself to excellence in clothing design and production. He was also the first to use mannequins to demonstrate his artistry. The clothing he designed was copied and sold around the world. Being the first, it can be justifiably claimed that he invented the international fashion industry.

Another old chestnut bandied about is that the English are happy to be good losers and lack the desire to win. This statement is hardly borne out by the facts. Quite a few of those who have made this remark have used, as comparison, some exceptional sporting performances by foreign athletes. Later findings have uncovered that some of the record breaking achievements have been fuelled by products emanating from world class chemical laboratories rather than dedicated human excellence. It might be worthwhile for people who make the 'happy to be losers' remark to remember that the climax of the 2004 Olympics saw the retirement of Steve Redgrave, an English sportsman who had won gold medals in every games spanning the previous 12 years and is regarded as one of the greatest Olympian athletes ever. He was partnered in his rowing events by others who had notched up achievements almost his equal.

We must admit that we are less successful when appointing those who run our sporting organisations. Our previously outstanding athletes, instead of being enlisted to train as coaches, trainers or administrators, are ignored Their knowledge and experience, instead of being directly conveyed to the current generation of burgeoning athletes is squandered, further contact with sport is usually confined to being commentators or journalists. Governing bodies show no sign of changing this patently faulty process, nevertheless our sports men and women are expected to produce superlative results.

In spite of them, over the years, we have managed to produce sporting icons of the calibre of Sebastian Coe, Jonathan Edwards, Daley Thompson, Brendan Foster, Steve Cram, Steve Ovett and Paula Radcliffe, some of whose records stood for decades. In world class sailing Alec Rose, Francis Chichester, winner of the first solo race across the Atlantic in 1931, and Ellen McArthur, the world record sailing heroine, are only a few whose successes stand as testimony. Our sailing and rowing teams have been dominant in the last three Olympics. Not a loser nor a drug taker amongst them. They epitomise all that we admire and, by delivering success, repudiate the good loser tag. Nevertheless the English media do seem to be happiest when highlighting failure, which tends to give the impression that winning everything should be regarded as an entitlement. Of course competitiveness and the pleasure of winning are inseparable, but should the imperative of winning come above all else? Is this not the philosophy which has diminished some of the pure enjoyment of sport and engendered the cult of the drug cheat?

Perhaps the English are better when acting individually than as team players, it does seem to be the case. When our competitors share control of their own preparation with the guidance of expert tutors they tend to excel more than under the supervision of committees. Some evidence of this may be gleaned from their achievements in boxing, rowing, cycling, sailing, golf and triathlon.

Too often in the past the English character has been identified to the world at large by its upper middle class or aristocracy, beginning with those who in the eighteenth and nineteenth centuries swanned through Europe on the Grand Tour with their immense wealth, siphoning up artistic treasures with which to adorn their country houses. A more accurate portrait of the people would have been gleaned from a study of middle-class entrepreneurship or the working class English artisan who, with innate inventiveness, started and then powered the industrial revolution. The ordinary people who, originally in pursuit of trade, took the first steps in building an empire throughout the world were not the same as those who, intent on power and control, later acted as its administrators and eventually soured it.

Probably because of the individuality and wide diversity of the English character, it is almost impossible to exemplify a definitive stereotype. It can range from Beatrix Potter to Stephen Hawking, Patrick Moore to Ken Dodd, Les Dawson to J.K. Rowling, Norman Wisdom to Enoch Powell or Andrew Lloyd Webber to Pam Ayres. It also produced ministers of religion like the Reverend Audley, who introduced children to his creation of Thomas the Tank Engine or Edmund Cartwright, another country parson, who, in the eighteenth century, invented a power loom for weaving even though he had never worked in the industry.

Our history of producing inventors is still undiminished,

recently demonstrated by James Dyson with a number of remarkable innovations and Trevor Bayliss, with his wind-up radio enabling millions of people in Africa, for the first time in their lives, to be in touch with the outside world. Perhaps Professor Ian Wilmut, the English scientist (of Dolly the Sheep fame) who discovered the method of cloning animals while he was working at a laboratory in Scotland or Tim Berners-Lee, who invented the World Wide Web are examples of this creativeness. The latter could have made him immensely rich but he decided that it should be available free for the benefit of everyone. Judge for yourselves, does 'unimaginative' describe the above?

Some English people complain that St George's Day is not commemorated more visibly, possibly by a programme on the BBC. The question arises: Why, and by what means? Perhaps a poet could qualify – but we have such a wealth of outstanding poets from which to choose, the arguments would be endless. Kipling, Milton, Donne, Clare, Browning, Masefield, Brooke, Byron, Keats and Geoffrey Chaucer are just a few. The differences arising from assessing their merits in some sort of priority would present an impossible task and could fragment quite a few friendships. Shakespeare is probably the best candidate, coincidentally he died on 23 April,* which coincides with St George's Day. That could present a problem because his work is being performed somewhere in the world almost on a daily basis. Dickens would have to be ruled out because, as the man who virtually invented the modern Christmas through his writing, he has carved his own niche in the consciousness of the nation and the world.

Another risible remark levelled against the English is that they are a mongrel race. Why should it be phrased in the

---

*The date of his birthday is not known for certain but he was baptized on the 26 April 1564 and a three day interval between birth and baptism was customary; because of this 23 April is the traditional date assigned to his birth.

form of an accusation or a slur – does anybody claim otherwise? In fact an Oxford professor has, as recently as 2006, published his findings based on extensive DNA analysis showing that the origins of the people of Britain generally, until 1950, have a great deal more in common with south-west Europe than was previously believed.

This mongrelism is something we have in common with a vast number of nations. Scotland is a mixture of English, Welsh, Irish, Scandinavian, Scots and Norman; probably Pict as well, although it is not entirely clear whether the Scots completely wiped them out in the tenth century. Wales was occupied by the Irish for a large part of the fifth century and the southern part of Wales so settled by English, Flemish and Normans in the eleventh century that it acquired the name of 'little England'. Ireland was invaded and settled by the Vikings for many generations and in the twelfth century by English and Welsh under the eponymous Norman marcher Lord Roger de Clare, Earl of Pembroke, who was invited in by Dermot, King of Leinster, for military assistance. Roger's payment was the hand in marriage to Dermot's daughter together with the right conferred on him to inherit the throne when the time came. Henry II did not agree with Dermot's action and took an army into Ireland to curb the ambitions of Roger when that inheritance came to fruition. Much of that army remained, presumably to become Irish. It also applies to the Jews, who spent hundreds of years settling in countries throughout Europe and inducting people into their society and religion. None of these incursions did any material harm to the indigenous populations or groups, in fact, it was probably more beneficial than continuous in-breeding. The famous historian H.A.L. Fisher, writing his comprehensive analysis of European history, states that 'Purity of race does not exist. Europe is a Continent of energetic mongrels.'

The subject of sexuality is another area where we have found ourselves under close and critical scrutiny. Even classic films such as *Brief Encounter*, made in 1945, have been used to portray the English as a sexually repressed nation. In their anxiety to prove the case the critics have missed the obvious. First it was not a documentary on the nation's attitude. It was a romantic story written and performed under the restrictions imposed by censorship of the time. It did not disguise the fact that the obstacles standing in the way of the couple, outweighed the opportunities available for the consummation of their feelings, thereby creating the tension sought by the producer. After all it was only a film! Its purpose was to make money not furnish an indicator of a nation's sexual proclivities. On the subject of sexual repression it might be remembered that, in the same year, Margaret Lockwood appeared in a fairly innocuous film, *The Wicked Lady*, which was banned for a time in the USA because she wore a dress with a neckline a couple of inches lower than they considered proper, so what conclusions may be drawn from this?

English Culture

To hear some drivel away about the decline in England and its culture one could easily gain an impression of a country on its last legs with nothing to offer, instead of the reality, which is quite the opposite. From top to bottom, England can compete on any level. From the rugged beauty of Northumberland which takes in Lindisfarne island and Durham Cathedral, encompassing the rich history of the northern counties to the exquisite mixture of mountain and pasture of the Cumberland Lake District it is breath-taking, as are the sweeping dales of north Yorkshire. Manchester, although principally noted for its part in the Industrial revolution, is home to the world famous Halle Orchestra. It also enjoys a prestigious musical reputation through its Royal College of

Music. In the centre of the city is located the magnificent Rylands Library containing many rare books and manuscripts, a fine museum and art gallery. The University has set standards of the highest quality and, as a constituent part, houses the Municipal College of Technology

On the way through the country there is a host of castles, stately homes and magnificent Norman cathedrals at which to marvel. The unrivalled picturesque villages of the Cotswolds, the houses built with timber frames and a delicate shade of stone, should not be by-passed. Add to these the counties of the south, south-east and south-west with excellent beaches and facilities for sailing, surfing, sea-fishing and camping. The attractions of London are enormously varied and it is probably the most cosmopolitan city in Europe. For theatregoers it is a magnet, staging world class musicals, ballet and theatrical plays regularly. The magnificent Natural History and Science Museums are unparalleled in their ability to ignite the imagination, especially of the young.

Some notable countrywide events taking place throughout the year forming part of English culture are Wimbledon, The Chelsea Flower Show, Crufts Dog Show Test Match cricket, Royal Ascot, The Derby, The Grand National, Cheltenham Festival, The Horse of the Year Show, The Boat Race, the Promenade concerts at the Albert Hall and the Boat Show, Cowes sailing week and the now revived annual Channel swimming race.

The foregoing is just an offering to counterbalance the gloomy impression sometimes conveyed by press reports. That so many people from all over the world seem keen to live in England may suggest that the inhabitants are not so bad after all. In spite of their foibles, weaknesses, eccentricities and occasional strengths, with perseverance in an effort to improve, they may one day equal the virtues of at least some of the critics.

Bibliography

British Encyclopedia (Odhams Press, 1933)

Bryant, Sir Arthur, *A History of Britain and the British People*
Vol 1 *Set in a Silver Sea* (HarperCollins, 1984)
Vol 2 *Freedom's Own Island* (HarperCollins, 1986)
Vol 3 *The Search for Justice* (HarperCollins, 1990)

Cassady, Richard F., *The Norman Achievement* (Sidgwick & Jackson, 1986)

Churchill, Winston S., *A History of English Speaking Peoples, Volume 1: The Birth of Britain* (1st ed. Dodd, Mead and Company, 1956; new ed., Weidenfeld & Nicolson, 2002)

Delderfield, Eric R., *Kings and Queens of England and Great Britain* (Weathervane Books, 1978)

Dictionary of National Biography (Oxford University Press)

Fisher, H.A.L., *A History of Europe* (Edward Arnold, 1936)

Fraser, Antonia, *Cromwell, our Chief of Men* (Weidenfeld & Nicolson, 1997)

Fruchtman, Jack, *Thomas Paine: Apostle of Freedom* (Four Walls Eight Windows, 1994)

Johnson, Paul, *The National Trust Book of British Castles* (Weidenfeld & Nicolson, 1978)

Lee, Christopher, *This Sceptred Isle 55 B.C. – 1901* (BBC Audiobooks, 1996)

Oman, Sir Charles, *A History of England before the Norman Conquest: Being a History of the Celtic, Roman and Anglo-Saxon Periods Down to the Year A.D. 1066* (1895; Methuen & Co., 1929)

213

Paxman, Jeremy, *The English: A Portrait of a People* (Michael Joseph Ltd, 1998)

Smiles, Samuel, *Men of Invention and Industry* (John Murray, 1884)
Lives of the Engineers (John Murray, 1904)
Industrial Biography; Iron Workers and Toolmakers (John Murray, 1908)

Sobel, Dava, *Longitude* (Fourth Estate, 1996)

Sumption, Jonathan, *The Hundred Years War, Vol 1 Trial by Battle* (Faber and Faber, 1990)

Tute, Warren, *The True Glory: Story of the Royal Navy* (Macdonald & Co, 1984)

Unstead, R.J., *Dictionary of History* (Ward Lock, 1976)

Warner, Philip, *The Daily Telegraph British Battlefields: The Definitive Guide to Warfare in England and Scotland* (Cassell Military Paperbacks, 2002)

Wormald, Patrick, *The Making of English Law, King Alfred to the Twelfth Century, Vol 1 Legislation and its Limits* (Wiley Blackwell, 1999)